Beautiful Life
BEYOND EXAMS

Beautiful Life BEYOND EXAMS

N. Raghuraman

Published by
PRABHAT PRAKASHAN PVT. LTD.
4/19 Asaf Ali Road,
New Delhi-110 002 (INDIA)
e-mail: prabhatbooks@gmail.com

ISBN 978-93-86231-03-1
BEAUTIFUL LIFE BEYOND EXAMS
by Shri N. Raghuraman

Edition
2026

Price
₹ 400.00 (Rupees Four Hundred only)

Printed at
Narula Printers, Delhi

Dedicated to my mother, Jayalaxmi Natarajan, who was my life coach and made me understand the real meaning of happy life and to my father, V. Natarajan, who anchored and steered my life to be financially successful.

Obviously this book is dedicated to all my teachers from Mrs. Saraswathi Kuppuswami and Lalita Ganesan at Saraswathi Vidyalaya, Nagpur to professors R.C. Bhargava and Sanjaya Gaur at IIT, Mumbai, where I last learnt as a student.

Am also indebted to my wife Premlata and daughter Nishevita who continues to give me life lessons by pushing me to embrace different roles in life.

Yes, learning never ends.

Open letter to my teachers

Some teachers go beyond their job descriptions. I remember when I first entered my school called Saraswathi Vidyalaya at Nagpur the first teacher was Mrs. Saraswathi Kuppuswami, who met my father for few seconds and took charge of me, maybe my life, held my hand and took me into her class. I looked back with teary eyes and as my father turned his back, may be he was uneasy in seeing me crying, I looked at my teacher's eyes. Her eyes had that assurance I needed her eyes had the love and the care I needed most. Since then I've never looked back. On that day, unknowingly, I learnt my first lesson—stand like a rock with love and care when somebody needs you the most.

She was not alone but there were many like her in that school and later on in my life too who did more than just teach the standard material required to pass the final examination. Year after year, they inspired me to overcome challenges, improved my life and helped me to accomplish my goals that I ever thought I would.

Dear teachers, let me confess here that I may not remember all the theories you taught me, despite the fact that I spent days studying them. But I remember the little stories that made the entire class laugh, I remember those silly biology projects in which the live frogs ran away from the laboratory, and I distinctly remember that remark, "ask questions, it is okay to ask silly questions and make silly mistakes."

This is what I took with me to my college and outside world. You have made a huge impact in my life and I am sure most of my peers who passed out from the school felt the same. I can also never forget my first principal, R D Swamy, despite being tough, she was godmother to many. In totality, you all inspired me and most of us to care for others with much compassion and love just as you taught us.

I want you all to know that I remember your compassion and your zeal and it is carried with me long after I passed out. I use these learnings to teach others in my own way. Hopefully, I will be happy if I achieve even half as much you had taught me.

Today, personally, I think it is Ok if your score card shows red marks provided if others go green by seeing you living your healthy and happy life.

I never would have been where I am today without that creative push from each one of you.

Yours
N. Raghuraman

Contents

1

Some people are never wrong in their life's mathematics

He was a Maths teacher with Saraswathi Vidyalaya, Nagpur. At least over 50,000 students might have got benefitted over four decades from him.

On January 2, few people gathered for this octogenarian's cremation. There was no pire, no pundits and no rituals and no running around. There was an uneasy calm.

Because the location for the cremation was the corridor outside the office of Dean of Anatomy's at Government Medical College, Nagpur. There were just few papers to be signed by the family. As the family bid final goodbye and silently nodded to the doctor the latter's eye met the helper's eye who was holding the stretcher and he rolled it wherein the lifeless body of Manohar S Kharkhanis was kept. The cremation got over.

Even after 40 years of teaching the teacher in him wasn't done teaching yet. He wanted his body to be pledged so that future anatomy students can learn even after he was gone. His lifeless body has gone into a post life-retirement job. His dedication and love to teaching doesn't come as a surprise to those who interacted with him in the school. And I was one of them in that school where I spent exactly a decade.

The first thing I always remember about him is self-reliance. He never made me to run to the teachers' room at the end of the long corridor to get few chalk pieces while entering our class room, while majority of my other teachers used to ask me to do that job, a job I hated all through my school life. That was because I was short in height, made to sit in the first bench just adjacent to the door.

The second thing that comes to me, is his smiling face and non complaining character.

He was the symbol of complete self-reliance and compassion. He allowed everyone of us ask questions and would patiently answer them.

Growing up in MP's Ujjain's bitter cold without a place to call home, Kharkanis could have had much to complain about in his life. For a man who grew up without parents and with just his brother to call family, Kharkanis ability to bind his own family so closely was even more amazing. And yet, he lived without any complaints and departed as a content man. His determination saw him fund his own education, raise a successful close-knit family in Nagpur, and send grandson to Harvard.

Kharkanis self-reliance was inspiring. I was told by his daughter Smita, who was my classmate, that he never sought help from anybody for his morning routines—waking up at 4.am, starting the water pump and preparing his own breakfast before his morning class—a routine he followed over 50 years.

In 2004 when his wife suffered a stroke and until 2013, when she died, Smita saw his infinite love for her mother which was evident in the way he forgot his own ailments as he attended to every smallest minute of her care. His utmost priority in those nine years was to live for his wife. He truly lived for his wife without a word of complaint. And three months after his wife left this world, he followed her, may be to take care his first love there but not before giving his body to his second love—students.

Funda is that some people have willpower to accept and to adjust to life's realities and it becomes a humbling lesson for most of us who have never faced the challenges. It is difficult to fill shoes of people like Kharkanis.

□

2

Mistakes makes you perfect!

Her name was Mrs. R.D. Swami. She was always referred as Swami Teacher, the principal of Saraswathi Vidyalaya at Nagpur in Maharashtra. She was the strictest teacher of my 20 years of education.

She used to carry the scale but never used. Her 5.10 inch height, well built body and her dark colour was enough to terrorise the "bad boys" of those years. She can make tough boys shiver by rolling her eyes. Parents love to have their children in that school only because of her.

When I started going to school at the age of six, I was forewarned about this tough lady and told that she is a zero tolerance teacher.

First day in the school she addressed us and told us that she does not teach to first standard students but will come and do surprise check of notebooks and home work. Nobody's notebook in that school ever escaped her red pen mark.

Year passed and the next year we started learning words, she entered the class and started telling us how we make small sentences. Later on my father told me that those sentences had dozen mistakes in spellings. But the markings on the side by Swami Teacher were always "good" to "very good". Sometimes I got even "wonderful".

I used to come back home and show it to my mother, who did not understand English and showed it to my father after he returns home with joy and he used to get mad on her. He used to say every sentence and every word that I wrote on the note book were wrong.

And my mother used to defend me saying that “if swami teacher has said good means it is good. In fact you know nothing about English”. My father, who had a command on English language always felt insulted after that argument but did not dare question Swami Teacher.

Wrong spellings and wrong grammar were regular on my notebook and one day my father could not tolerate and took the notebook from me and walked into her cabin. I was not there to listen to their conversation. But after that he never said a word about my writing. Years passed by, I also forgot the issue. Finished my education, became a journalists and one day in Mumbai we received the news of her death.

The curiosity in me suddenly forced me to ask my father what was the conversation between her and him then. He said in verbatim: Natti, (my father name is natarajan and was referred by close people as Natti) Don’t you think I know English better than you? I know they are wrong. All of them in the class are wrong when it comes to any language, not only English. But the children are just beginning to get excited about writing words, forming sentences and all of them are not with just mistakes but with blunders. If I put my red pen on their copy, I would be dampening the spirit of writing. I will be killing the bud before it bloom and start loving words. Let them fall in love with words. Spellings and grammars can wait. I don’t want them to hate words that have red ink marks.

Funda is that when you introduce something new any human being of any age, never go with the 'do and don't list'. That will dampen the spirit of loving that product or learning. Encourage them to embrace the new thing and then correct it en route.

□

3

Higher education is certainly not only for procuring job

Academically excellent people choosing a career other than job is less heard of. And if any one of us had scored like Akash Majumdar, who topped this year in GMAT exam, we would be dreaming of entering an organisation that will envy the world.

Early this week, Akash had scored 770 out of 800, which is the highest in India till now this year. Reports earlier suggested that Annie Manjila of Christ University, Bengaluru scored 760 at GMAT this year, which was the highest. But Akash's score has bettered with his percentile being at 99.

His SAT score was 2,380 out of 2,400. He finished his schooling at The Calcutta International School, where he was first-class first all through, but also was head-boy and developed interest in several extracurricular activities, including music.

With GMAT score, he can choose to get admitted in any of the global top colleges, like Harvard, Stanford or Oxford universities. On an average, scores of 690, 725 and 733 are needed to get admitted into Oxford, Harvard and Stanford universities respectively. This GMAT score is valid for five years from now, before which he can seek admission for his MBA course.

He is just 19 and is already majoring in economics at Vanderbilt University, USA, that too through scholarship. He had a natural aptitude for economics and mathematics that he was able to comprehend tough theories and problems with ease.

On reading about Akash's brilliance, majority of us will think that God has been kind on him and he will be picked up by any international giants at a very high package after his professional course.

But if you ask Akash, he is not in a rush to choose any of these renowned universities until he is clear which university will help him teach not only the professional MBA course but also help him provide a platform to launch his own music label in Kolkata.

Yes, Akash is passionate about music. Piano is his life. For Akash, who solves difficult maths problems and plays piano with equal ease, music is something that runs in his DNA, which he claims to have inherited from his maternal grandfather.

For academically excelled people, becoming front-runner is less heard of. He is grade 8 certified pianist under the Associated Board of Royal School of Music and Trinity College, London. His dream is not only to launch his own label of music but want to make that label as a platform for those who are really talented but less known and underprivileged musicians. For him, nothing matches his passion for music.

He is very clear that he will use all his academic knowledge in the classroom to help build his own music label. It is not that he will not take up a job in the future or not, but he certainly knows what he wants to do with his education and nurture his passion too. The clarity at this young age makes Akash stand out in the crowd.

Youngsters generally assume that higher education is a gateway to their dream job. It is also actually a window to tap your own potential and passion. Job and/ or chasing your passion are some of the options among many. Choose what suits you best.

Funda is that use your higher education for opening your wisdom basket within you and help yourself choose the best in your life and follow your passion.

□

4

You can repair a man's life like machines

Dev Kumar Vishvakarma was the only able member of that family. Father had abandoned him, his aged mother and young polio-affected brother. After 10th, 'Deva', as he was fondly called, true to his name, shouldered that responsibility and took care of the basic living.

But fate had another plan. He became mentally unstable, started roaming around the Mopka's Raj Kishore Nagar of Bilaspur, in semi-nude condition. Abusing everyone passing through was a regular affair, and people felt pity.

The only person with whom he was calmer was Vijay Kumar Zade, the owner of Asha Auto Care and his eight workers, who had some soft corner for this unkept young man. Initially, they helped with money. He ignored their readiness to offer him a job and Deva slowly became a parasite to all in that area. And that was the time his well-wishers took control of the situation.

Vijay and his mechanics Sahu, Raghu, Golu, Dileep, Shani, Yasin one day planned to take him to Shendari Government Mental Hospital and the hospital refused to admit him since none of them was Deva's relative. After hours of persuasion and making Deva's mother as witness, the treatment began, but Deva used to run away from the hospital often, only to be brought back by these friends.

It was not much money that they had donated for Deva's welfare and treatment but they donated certainly a lot of time in treating and monitoring him on a daily basis. Years of their hard work finally paid fruit five months ago. Deva had come back as a normal person but the problem before him was none wanted to give him any employment.

Vijay again came forward and trained him as a helper to all his eight mechanics. Today, if you happen to visit Asha Auto Care, you will hear, "Deva, get that spanner number 8; Deva, push the oil can; Deva, wash this oil from this screw." The name of Deva will echo from all sides of the workshop and a young man will be running helter-skelter, helping each of the mechanics with no reaction. For Deva, each one of them has done something to make his life better. The work in the auto care and the companionship of eight people has given a sense of meaning to Deva today.

Five weeks of training have made him a great helper and his weekly salary is taking care of the family's hunger, that was reduced to penury not long before. Since the last three months, Deva comes back every week after his salary-day and give complete accounts on what he spent his earnings to Vijay and his mechanic friends. And when he says, "I brought the complete ration for the week" or when he says, like a three-year-old kid happy on the newly acquired toy, "after a long time, I tasted non-vegetarian dish cooked by my mother," tears roll-out from those young nine pairs of eyes and they feel proud that they not only help in setting the car machines right, but somewhere they managed to set the human life in a running condition after it got junked ten years before.

Khalil Gibran has said once, “How can I lose faith in the justice of life when the dreams of those who sleep upon feathers are not more beautiful than the dreams of those who sleep upon the earth?”

Funda is that repairing machines and putting them back on running condition is easy for us humans, but only few among us can apply that logic to human life.

□

5

Sarkari school ke malik hum hai bhagwan nahi!

Early morning a WhatsApp message dropped into my inbox from our Udaipur-based Dainik Bhaskar reader, Naveen Pandya saying that most of the graduates in his state do not know the difference between woman and women, which are basic English. Barring a few, pass-outs even from graduates of private institutions make silly mistakes. So, one can understand the level of state-run institutions. "In fact, सरकार का तो भगवान् ही मालिक है..." he concluded.

It brought a huge smile on my face because I was entering the office of the directorate of Education of a state; the name of the state, please don't ask.

While the meeting went on the quality of education for a longer duration, his departmental officers kept on intervening – some for the director's signature and some for getting his ratification on the decision they want to take.

One such conversation surprised me. The Junior officer said that bringing new table and chair for every teacher in every room of every newly opened government schools is next to impossible since the budget allocated for the purpose is too small. The director asked him what is the alternate to this situation?

The officer's face glowed, since he was considered worthy to comment on the situation; pat came the reply.

With an authority on the subject, he said, "Sir, half of the teachers in government schools anyway do not attend school. Besides, if their job is to teach subjects, why should the government should provide them chairs?" Since the director did not show any reaction on his face, he added two bits of his own opinion, "after all, our job is to help education and not teachers."

The director looked at my face. I pretended to be busy on my phone that was silent and he told his officer, "Come out with some more options too. I will discuss it with you after lunch."

After his departure, I insisted that we both step out for a cup of coffee and that too to Starbucks. A very honest officer politely declined my offer but I prevailed on him saying that the outing may give some food for thought for his post-lunch meeting on classroom accessories.

We both reached Starbucks and there was a long queue and we decided to take the table after getting our respective coffee. While standing, I made the director to ask the person behind the counter in their local language accent that "don't they get tired standing all day?" The young was quick in his response. He called the director behind the counter and showed him a mat on which he was standing. And said, "Standing for long periods of time is an unfortunate reality in our business. But, by using these anti-fatigue mats, it first reduces back, foot and leg pain; promotes good blood circulation; reduces our fatigue from hard surfaces; reduces slip and fall injuries besides protecting the dropped breakables." He said all in one breath. And, finally, he said one-liner, "Sir, these mats cost in thousands."

We picked up our coffee with a smile and started discussing on why government teachers always complain and he himself came out with an answer by saying,

"Maybe because they suffer back pain and joint soreness since they stand on cement or a tile whole day and they eventually attract more physical ailments. Happy employees have happy interactions and pass positive vibrations, he said. I felt happy for providing that food for thought; it gets applied or not is a different issue.

Funda is that if you care for your teachers, they will care for their students. Why bring Bhagwan into that?

□

6

Faith and abundance are twins

Moral Story: Once a man got lost in a desert. With no water for the last two days, he dragged himself to an abandoned hut. He entered it and to his surprise, he saw handpump and started working on it in vain. He was exhausted in a while.

Then the man noticed a bottle in one corner of the hut. It was filled with water and corked up to prevent evaporation. He uncorked the bottle and was about to gulp down the sweet life-giving water, when he noticed a piece of paper attached to it. Handwritten on the paper read: "Use this water to start the pump. Don't forget to fill the bottle when you're done."

He had a dilemma. He could follow the instruction and pour the water into the pump, or he could ignore it and just drink the water. What to do? If he let the water go into the pump, what assurance did he have that it would work? What if the pump malfunctioned? What if the pipe had a leak? What if the underground reservoir had long dried up? But then... maybe the instruction was correct. Should he risk it? If it turned out to be false, he would be throwing away the last water he would ever see. Faith took over his thoughts. Hands trembling, he poured the water into the pump. Then he closed his eyes, said a prayer, and started working on the pump. He heard a gurgling sound, and then water came gushing out, more than he could possibly use.

He filled his flask for the journey ahead. He also filled the bottle and put the cork back in. Before leaving the hut, he added his own writing below the instruction: "Believe me, it works!"

Real Story: Students from 45 hamlets in the village of Hamirpura under the Laxmangarh tehsil in Sikar at Rajasthan were unable to go to well-maintained Shahid Rajendra Singh Government Senior Secondary School, due to lack of conveyance, despite the fact that the school was in the 3 km-radius.

So, the villagers collected money, purchased a bus, and gifted it to a government school for ferrying students last week. They also showed their willingness to pay for driver's salary and fuel expenses.

They felt that though there is no guarantee that all children will willingly go to school if the bus starts operating, the village elders felt that conveyance cannot be an excuse to any student for missing education, it can at least become an attraction and convenience.

Sikar students faring well in the class tenth results of Rajasthan Board of Secondary Education this year also inspired the gesture.

Three villages, Kantewa, Manasia and Jasarasar, that are about 5 to 7 km far from the school have also been connected now due to this new initiative. Currently, majority of the children are students studying in classes I to V.

It is good to see that villagers have the faith that this gesture will make the next generation educated, surely more than they are. Ratan Singh Shekhawat, an ex-serviceman and sarpanch of Hamirpura village, contributed ₹ 1.51 lakh and rest of the money was collected by villagers. Today, every child in that village goes to school due to this initiative. And there was sparkling smile like the new bus on the parents' face when the bus came calling on this weekend.

Funda is that faith plays an important role in giving, besides telling us indirectly that unless you give something first, nothing will come back in abundance.

□

7

Emotions and technology are pair of rails to successful business

Sahil Sani is not a techie and a student of liberal arts. One day he sat down before a shopkeeper and the conversation he had hit him very badly. The shopkeeper said, "We pull up our shutters every morning to do business like our father and grandparents did. At the end of the day, we close the shop and take the cash home, which is just behind. Nothing has changed for over hundred years."

He also expressed that the shop was set by his forefathers for a small family, but with increasing number of family members, more people started living from the income of the same shop, thus affecting cash flow, ability to stock more or add variety of goods.

This set Sahil to think who then met hundreds of such retailers and shopkeepers and realised that there is a strong sense of agitation or feeling of being left out from the modern world in them and instantly he got an idea to do business only meant for the roadside shopkeepers.

After joining hands with Bharat Balachandran, they went to launch "Just Buy Live" an app that allows these extra members of shopkeepers to branch out and become sub distributors for Just Buy and add to the family income.

Launched in January 2016, this app has added over 2,500 brands and 3,00,000 products. The App is designed in such a way that a retailer can see all the brands available, stock-keeping units like 100-grams pocket to a large kilogram pockets, the retailer margin, the maximum retail price, delivery schedules and the credit limit he or she can enjoy.

The App has a credit product called 'udhaar', which offers retailers structured credit lines for their stock-in-trade requirements.

The differentiation for this e-distributor is that they are able to empower India's least or unempowered community called 'retailers', Sahil claims.

Terming their business as the starting of 'Aam dukandar movement', he says it helps any member retailer of Just Buy to call on a tollfree number, where an accounts manager helps out with questions and answers and takes the retailer through the steps of ordering stocks or understanding various offers on the product.

With one click, Sahil claims to have wiped out several layers of margin system in which the retailer who is successful in selling the products gets the least profit.

The direct fallout of this move is that today a member retailer picks up his smart phone, checks his available credit limit and margins in each brand, corelate them to his market demand and order stocks from each brand. For you and me, it doesn't look new and may ask, "So, what's new in that?" But for the retailer who has been ordering stocks, the way his grandfather was ordering, now embracing technology is certainly a new thing.

India is rapidly moving into the mobile app age and is already the fourth largest mobile app economy. In 2016, it is estimated that app downloads would reach 7.7 billion and set to grow to 29.1 billion by 2020.

Time spent on smart mobile apps, particularly in relation to retail shopping apps by each Indian, grew by

11.5 percent, driven by e-commerce majors like Snapdeal, Amazon, Flipkart among many. With buyers heavily and steadily moving into apps, millions of retailers are also catching up this phenomenon by regrouping themselves or joining big brands to encase the trend.

Funda is that future businesses are going to be technology-driven, but it cannot run without understanding the emotions of a particular community for whom and with whom you want to do business.

□

8

Sensitive people make this planet a better place to live in

It was pouring all throughout the day and somewhere late evening, a Mumbaikar, Usha Pratap, was travelling on the Mumbai-Pune express highway. While she was basically enjoying the lush green of the ghats and her car wiper's dance to the rain, she suddenly saw a state transport-run bus overtaking her car and travelling at a high speed.

She was not annoyed the way the bus threw up all the water collected on the road on her car since that has been the norm of many drivers in our country but she was frightened the way the bus was wobbling and moving at a high speed.

Her lips prayed for all passengers inside the bus but her wisdom and intelligence said somebody should be informed about this mad driver and somebody should also stop this maddening speed, since this highway is notoriously known for fatal accidents, at least in the recent past.

For a commoner like Usha, obviously, no senior persons' name from the transport organisation came to mind. However, she put her leg on the accelerator, came close to the bus, noted the number, parked her car on the side and directly tweeted to the Chief Minister of Maharashtra, Devendra Fadnavis and Nitin Gadkari, the Union Minister for Surface Transport. Usha was happy that as a responsible citizen, this is what she can do – raising the concern to the highest level.

One will appreciate that Usha either knew the driver nor wanted any revenge with him. It was her fear that nothing should happen to those poor passengers plying on the bus.

Around 90 minutes later, she gets a reply from none other than Fadnavis himself. His first word was "apologies" and then he continued "action will be taken against the bus driver Sandip after due enquiry." Understanding the sensitivity of the tweet, which is safety of those unknown passengers for Usha and her followers, Fadnavis added a beautiful line to that tweet, which read as "Bus reached safely to Pune at 8:45 p.m."

This reminds me of a story from Mahabharata wherein once Arjuna asked Lord Krishna why he called Yudhishtira Dharamaraj, and Karna Daanveer. To answer this question, Krishna disguised himself and Arjuna as Brahmins and decided to visit both the kings. On visiting Yudhishtira, they asked for sandalwood pieces to perform Havan. Since it was raining heavily at the time, the soldiers sent by Yudhishtira couldn't find dry sandalwood suitable to be used as a fuel. While he was thinking what to do next, both went to Karna and asked for the same thing. Karna searched everywhere for dry sandalwood but failed. But, he did not let the Brahmins go home empty-handed. He picked up his sickle, cut his darbar's doors made of sandalwood, telling them that he would get his door remade when he finds the sandalwood.

Now, Krishna tells Arjuna that if you had asked for Yudhishtira's darbar's door, also made of sandalwood, he would have given that without hesitation. "Karna is Daanveer because he thinks beyond the normal thinking pattern," he concludes.

On Monday, when I was on my way to attend the Dainik Bhaskar Knowledge Series at Panipat via New Delhi, I happened to see a news item there. Delhi's Deputy Chief Minister, Manish Sisodia announced that motorists obstructing the way of ambulances carrying patients to hospitals in the National Capital Region would have to pay a penalty of ₹ 2,000 and requested citizens to be sensitive towards such emergency situations. The insensitive attitude of few forced this action.

Funda is that it is only sensitive people who make this planet a better place to live in and than glittering gigantic infrastructure.

□

9

Hard work has its own charm

Story 1: When PSLV C-34 rocket with 20 satellites lifted off successfully at 9.25 a.m. on June 22 this year from Sriharikota in Andhra Pradesh, there were shouts from as far as the terrace of Sathyabama University in Chennai. Some groups of students ran out to look at the clear blue sky to see the telltale white streak as the rocket zoomed to place the satellites in their orbits.

That is because one of the satellites weighing 1.592 kg, SATHYABAMASAT, on which the students have worked since 2010 to monitor greenhouse gas concentration in the atmosphere was part of the project. Many students have been part of it, which spanned over six years, before the present batch gave final shape to all their aspirations. The students find it hard to believe that something they created, touched and felt is now up there.

Of the 12 people, including two girls, in the project, we meet six—four from Andhra Pradesh, and one each from Telangana and Odisha respectively. The others have graduated; some have stayed back to help the core team that went to Bengaluru for the final two-odd months. And almost all of them were from small towns.

The satellite has a life span of six months. After that, it will be decommissioned. The data from the satellite will be shared to help curb environmental degradation. For the teachers who stayed with the students in Bengaluru, it was a chance to share ideas outside of the classroom, and engage in a healthy discussion. For parents, who were worried about their children working non-stop, seeing their children make news was an emotional moment and the result of that hard work.

Even Prime Minister, Narendra Modi made specific mention of the students in his monthly 'Mann Ki Baat'. Former Union Human Resource Development Minister, Smriti Irani called up one of the team members and wished them.

Story 2: At least twice a week, he goes for six hours of dialysis, which includes travel time to his house and back, which is one hour more than the time he spent in his school as a teacher but this 32-year-old dedicated faculty of St. Stephen's School, Bowbazar, Kolkata never cited this as a reason and took off since 2008, when he was diagnosed with renal failure, and since he began this routine, not even one day he took off despite he was eligible, at least, for his paid holidays.

The commerce graduate was working with a coal merchant's office since 2005. His job forced him to travel every part of the north-east besides Madhya Pradesh and Odisha and his illness forced him to quit. Ailment invaded his body almost silently.

Joined school, but there are many days when his blood pressure shoots up and he starts throwing up. Yet, Pappu Roy does not have the luxury of ending his day at 4 p.m., which is when school gets over. He heads straight to a coaching institute to teach privately before returning to his home at 8 p.m., where another batch of students would be waiting for him.

Each dialysis session costs him ₹ 1,450, taking his total expenditure close to ₹ 15,000, besides arranging blood transfusion for himself. He works hard not only to pay for the mounting bills but for, most of the time, the work pressure, the smiling faces of the children, young student's curiosity to know better on the subjects he teaches makes him forget his own pain and worries.

Funda is that hard work has no specific definition to explain, since it has different meanings for different people, but it has its own charm that always has to be experienced.

□

10

Do 'shadow job' to get best insight

What is shadow job?: A group of 11 US pre-medical students are currently in Ahmedabad practising 'shadow physician' on a 15-day foreign exchange programme, that enables them to observe the public health infrastructure in the third-world countries. Everyday they follow a doctor and observe the daily routine in different wards. They were astounded by the large number of patients treated at government hospitals with minimum resources. According to them, 15-day 'shadow-jobbing' has given them more knowledge than the entire medical course.

Takehome: Every young Indian entering a new career must do this 'shadow-jobbing' not only in his/her area of work, but I suggest they must practise this 'shadowing' in at least three more areas—**innovation, dedication and perseverance**—since these are common qualities to any profession. Here are some examples.

Innovation: Students of Patna's Birla Institute of Technology have developed a Formula One car to take part in Supra SAE (Society of Automotive Engineers) India 2016. A 20-member team, which calls itself 'Thunderbolt', has developed the single-seater racing car. The event was held at the Buddha International Circuit from July 4 to July 9 in 2016. The competition, into its fifth year, tests skills of automobile enthusiasts across the country.

Headed by Abhinash Panda, a fourth-year mechanical engineering student, the team is divided into four departments—designing, suspension, transmission and marketing—and then started working on designs. The college provided a well-equipped laboratory to carry out fabrication and it took three months to develop the car. There are three rounds—technical inspection in which features of a car are inspected, static round in which presentations on various parts of a car are made, and dynamic event where a car's acceleration and braking systems are tested. Only after clearing these stages, a vehicle be allowed to appear in the final race.

Dedication: Gajendragad, which is 418 kms from Bengaluru and is well-known for long beautiful hill strips that house several historical forts. That is the reason when 50-year-old Suresh B Chalageri got transferred as a teacher to this place, he could not find the sole government Byrapura Lower Primary School with 60 students, mostly shepherd's children. Local shepherd said that trekking eight kms is the only way to reach the school. And Suresh took up the job because he felt those kids needed him. He acted as a principal, teacher, head peon and also watchman. Now it is seven years and nine months, he continues to act like that the students' numbers never shrunk.

This dedicated teacher treks everyday to reach his destination, sometimes carrying books and foodgrains, traversing a distance of 8 km. In fact, he is the sole reason that Byrapura Lower Primary School is still running.

Perseverance: The compost produced from wet waste at Bengaluru-based IT professional, Clement Jayakumar's kitchen is used in his terrace garden for the past eight years, everyday. Today the fifty bags placed in his garden grow vegetables. like tomato, ladies' finger and beans among many and his entire family's vegetable needs are taken care of.

Inspired by him and the taste of organic vegetables, almost all of Clement's neighbours too have begun composting wet waste and growing veggies and the whole colony of 1,000 households practises it today. Neither is it expensive nor cumbersome. Once used to it, it just becomes a part of routine and takes 15 minutes a day besides avoiding one truck load of waste from each house each year.

Funda is to do a shadow-job of your choice to get the best insight of the career that you are going to embrace for life.

□

11

Positive thinking takes you miles ahead of others

He is from Saharanpur, UP. Like any other young, at the age of 23, he is bright, ambitious, loves sports, remains hooked to movies and English TV serials, and leaps at the opportunity of any road trip. It was a tough decision for him to leave his comfort zone, his own city for a reason that you would be shocked to know. But he decided against the odds and left home to do his graduation from the famous Shri Ram College of Commerce, New Delhi. His journey did not end there. He moved on from there to join Indian Institute of Management, Bengaluru.

Today, he is an inspiration for everyone in that college. There is not a single student in that campus who does not know him. What makes him inspiring and perhaps more popular is that unlike those of us who falter at the slightest sight of adversity, he is a fighter. He strongly believes that whatever happens to you or in anybody's life, it is temporary. He advocates that life must go on and one must move ahead irrespective of hurdles, failures and even loss of some parts of the body.

What you wouldn't have guessed so far is that this IIM student, Kshitiz Aneja is a double amputee, elbow down and he not only knows perfectly but also taught himself to live a life as normal as anybody else. Kshitiz lost his hands when he was just 8 years old, but he survived high school, college and is now in one of the most prestigious institutes of India.

Kshitiz got back to school a year after he met with the accident. There were people who were sceptical about it, but his parents believed otherwise. His mother used to accompany him to school until he taught himself to write. His friends were very supportive and welcomed him back to school. Teachers were more than helpful. And this boy went on to score an 86 per cent in Class 10 and a 91 per cent in Class 12. That is when he decided to shift to New Delhi for graduation, a decision most of the kith and kin were unsure since he was completely dependent on his family. That is when he took a one-year break, tried living on his own in Delhi for three months, like a probation time. He fared alright and decided to go on with it. Today, when he decided to move to Bengaluru to join IIM, the same relatives and friends knew he would do it without any trouble.

He plays football, writes, uses technology and wants to travel at least 200 countries in the next ten years to find out how this world is treating people like him. And he knows that he can achieve that by excelling academically.

Always cheerful, never seeking sympathy, Kshitiz has major plans to open a website to motivate other such affected people and currently works with an NGO that helps rehabilitate amputees. He also teaches at the institute's weekend classes for children of non-teaching staff.

Kshitiz taught himself to be independent. Even without a tool, he is able to write and type, use a camera since photography is one of his hobbies and do almost everything on his own.

A crowd-funded documentary film based on his life is in its preliminary stages. The documentary, directed by

Keshav Kalra of New India Films, is an attempt to spread the encouraging message of Kshitiz's life, especially among those in a similar predicament.

Funda is that no life is without hurdles but your positive thinking can easily take you miles ahead of others.

□

12

Life is never secured in a wrong designation

I know Mukesh Patil (name changed) for a long time. Fairly good at studies, although my rating is mediocre, he has been the first post-graduate in the village of 5,000 people. The entire village had appreciated him by felicitating him at various forums and also frequently called him in public meetings to motivate their student community. These public appreciations, felicitations over a period of time had made him highly opinionated and he had a viewpoint in almost everything. Unfortunately, he puts his opinion with a bit of aggression without substantial support of facts and figures. In fact, sometimes I call him eccentric and he seldom believed in listening. He offers his opinion without asking for it and all his observations had been negative.

As some real friends distanced from him, he found Facebook as the medium for expression with virtual friends. Strongly worded opinions got him more 'likes' since we as Indians somehow unite in condemning anything and unfortunately Mukesh thought these virtual followers are his real friends.

On the other hand, this one-up manship with negativity had failed him in all personal interviews despite the fact that he had managed to clear most written examinations.

This 'know-all' young man felt that he is fit for only government jobs, and he started hunting vigorously for it.

Recently, the Maharashtra Public Service Commission (MPSC) advertised for five 'hamal' (porters) posts. Mukesh, a post-graduate, is also an applicant. The advertisement clearly said that the minimum educational qualification for the post is just fourth-standard pass and the age-limit is 18 to 33 and they have to appear for simple written test for their basic linguistic and mathematics abilities. The job offered a salary of between ₹ 13,000 and ₹ 14,000 per month.

The MPSC received exactly 2,424 applications, which is not surprising, considering people like Mukesh are also applicants. Of the total applications, 5 are MPhil holders, 9 are PG Diploma holders, 109 are Diploma holders, 253 are PG Degree holders, 984 are graduates, 605 are HSC passed, 282 are SSC passed and only 177 are below 10th-standard passed but none are just fourth-standard passed.

In normal circumstances, the MPSC has to conduct a simple written test followed by a simpler interview with basic physical test. But now they need to conduct the same written exam for all 2,424 applicants; since most of them will easily passes the interviews, according to the MPSC secretary, Rajendra Mangrulkar, is going to be far more tougher than they anticipated, since he feels that the anxiety to have a secured government job has driven so many well educated young Indians to embrace a job for which they are overqualified.

Mukesh initially defended his decision for taking up porter's job. But, slowly, he realised that his real and virtual followers have distanced themselves saying that "if one has to take up a job meant for less educated, then what good this higher education does?" He felt that village people were not giving him that second look that they used to give last year.

Mukesh has suddenly become sensitive to these observations and he is being seen withdrawing himself from all activities – real and virtual, and a feeling of insecurity has slowly creeped into this young 24-year-old. Now he is not sure that he will appear for MPSC written exam and subsequent interview slated to be held this August.

Funda is that life is never secured in a wrong designation or wrong packaging. Make sure you have the right job for sustainability. It doesn't matter it is government or private.

□

13

Every small contribution to the society's good is too big

Story 1: She is just 23-year-old young but 84 percent physically challenged. Her father runs a small shop at Thane near Mumbai after his accident while being an auto-rickshaw driver and mother supplements the household income by being a tailor.

Diksha Dinde pursuing her masters in history is suffering from cerebral palsy quadriparxsis since birth but has not let his disability come in her way of her desire to educate underprivileged children who do not go to school for various reasons and she is doing this for over four years.

Diksha who can't move without help due to her spinal cord problem is keen to create a world of children, who are not afraid of going to school for some reasons.

And in November 2015, Diksha will be the only Indian to be selected for United Nations' "A world at school" program and will be visiting Washington DC to share her idea with ambassadors of other countries. Every year, UN selects 500 ambassadors on the basis of their work in the field of education.

Story 2: An Ambassador, that too of a country like Mexico, which is 15th largest economy of the world with per capita GDP of $10,307.28 against India's per capita

GDP of $1,498.97 is concerned about the pollution. Since she is an ambassador to India, she goes to her workplace daily in New Delhi in an auto-rickshaw specially painted in floral blue for her. She dumped her Mercedes and BMWs and chose auto because she felt that it was way of contributing to Delhi's air quality.

Story 3: When all children would like to sleep at the crack of dawn, a bunch of young kids at UP's Mawaiya village in Mirzapur quietly spreaded out and hided in the tree branches, bushes and abandoned houses to spot anyone headed to the fields to defecate by blowing whistles and driving them away. Named as Bal Nigrani Samiti, they also put the offender's name in small flag and place it near the faeces. This was just the beginning to shame the villagers and make them think about toilets. This effort has led several blocks of Mirzapur district to be declared as the first open defecation-free village. The results are discernible – this summer there has been no diarrhoea cases, less flies and overall good health for villagers.

Story 4: Pipantola is one small village among thousands in Chhattisgarh with just 25 to 30 houses that were hit by severe drought. The protected Baiga tribe saw their small subsistence crop fail. This April, with the help of an NGO, they began a community well from scratch without any government help. They kept digging everyday after their work and hopes were beginning to fade until they reached 40 feet deep, since they saw no water. And, suddenly, at 41st feet, they stuck water. Now they knew that the well could hold the rain-water now and there would be no drought the next year.

After their success, the local administration suddenly woke up from their deep slumber and started digging wells in other places to prove a point in their favour. But hundreds of villages in the surrounding areas have come to know that they can do anything for their survival without anybody's help. Risk taken to dig one well on their own has boosted the courage of other villagers.

Funda is that no contribution is small if it is done with a good intention and for the betterment of tomorrow's society and its comparison with each other is unjustified. Every little contribution matters to the human race in totality.

□

14

Nothing can stop determination

Story 1: They are the most unprivileged lot; so seeing even football was not possible, forget playing the game. They have never seen any other locality other than they are born in, forget about country, airport or plane. Being the children of a watchman or some workers in a factory, their best leisure was a dose of various gully games including cricket using the aerated bottles' crate as their stumps. But, today, Aruna Chauhan, Jalpa Parmar, Sunita Raval and Karina Bhatti from Thaltej Primary School No. 1 and Gopal Thakor and Rohankumar Solanki from Jodhpur Prathamik Shala No. 1 all from Ahmedabad are now excited to take part in the seven-a-side soccer tournament along with students from over 300 schools from across the globe and are going to represent their country in Sweden in the Gothia Cup.

Story 2: For years, he studied in his mud house with no electricity braving the temperature close to 50 degrees Celsius and during night under a lantern on a tree at the village chaupal. During winters, when the temperature would dip drastically, son of daily-wage agricultural labourer, Pabulal, of nondescript Chokla village in Barmer of Rajasthan. Pabulal would sit at the chaupal with just a thin blanket so that the warmth of the blanket wouldn't put him to sleep. And he secured

116 all-India rank in OBC category of All India Institute of Medical Sciences (AIIMS). And he doesn't think electricity, bedroom, laptop, music and de-stressing exercises are required to clear any exam. He believes that all one needed is presence of mind, who prepared for medical examination with the help of villagers.

Pabulal was helping his parents in the field when he got to know his results. He didn't leave the work until evening to ensure full wages. His life took a new turn when his uncle offered help for his education and shifted to Barmer. He is currently trying to have at least two pairs of trousers and shirts so that he can look presentable in AIIMS along with other students.

Story 3: Each year, their native village of about 400 families in Bihar floods over as the River Bagmati swells with the monsoon. The two come from a family of seven. Growing up, the family was so hard-pressed that fullsome meals could not be taken for granted.

The 19-year-old Krishna Kumar grew up in Paroria village, Samastipur, Bihar, where the younger one would carry his older brother to school because he had lost the use of his legs to polio. Now, both have reason to celebrate as they have cleared the JEE (Advanced) with the older brother ranked 38th all-India in the OBC Persons with Disability category, younger brother secured the 3,675 rank in OBC category.

Story 4: Being born in Bihar probably, it gave that grit and courage and standing up for her rights since these attributes can't always be developed with training. From the ramp (modelling) to the examination hall, she made a mark everywhere. She was a meticulous and committed with high ability to overcome challenges during her BE project. No wonder she got scholarship for six consecutive semesters. She completed her engineering in medical electronics in 2014 and aimed to fulfil her life-long dream of flying. Meet Bhawana Kanth – one of the first three women fighter pilots of the Indian Air Force (IAF) on this Saturday along with Flying Officers Mohana Singh and Avani Chaturvedi. Bhawana did it all because she was determined.

Funda is that nothing can stop determined minds to achieve its goal; in fact, God helps them.

□

15

Good communication is like icing on a cake

Denua is a small village with just 218 families and with a population of 1,010 people situated at Ghagarbeda tehsil of Mayurbhanj district in Odisha. Despite no major emphasis on education, it is one of the few Indian villages where females outlive males with 2011 population reading 498 males against 512 females. That is because males have lost lives to various unrelated incidents.

Rajanikant Nayak is one such person, who lost his father in early childhood and his mother is a daily-wage labourer and the family's sole earning member. His only sister suffers from paralysis and is bed-ridden. The entire family and village do not even know the exact disease she is suffering from. She had discontinued her studies after Class 5 due to this medical problem.

For kids like Rajanikant, the motivational stories include successful life stories of engineers and doctors, whom village leaders, seniors and parents meet during their visit to the nearby towns. These children always want to become somebody like in the real story people narrate. But none says how to become one. Since somebody told him that good score will make him a doctor or engineer, and for that he needs to study hard, Rajanikant has developed a habit of studying eight to nine hours a day since there is nothing much to do in that village that would distract from his focus.

The only good thing the mother did was that she got him admitted to local Kendua primary school in her own village which was up to Class 5. Later, the teachers helped him enroll in a school run by the SC/ST development department which had a residential facility. That solved many problems of him, primarily the poverty. Since he scored 89.9 percent in the matriculation examination, the teachers helped him join the Kalinga Institute of Social Sciences (KISS) for his plus-two junior college. There the teachers coached him for JEE (advanced).

All these struggles did not make the 17-year-old Class 12 student Rajanikant any less to metro students. He cracked the JEE (Advanced) by securing an all-India ST rank of 245. The lack of knowledge is so high at his home and village that when he said he cracked JEE advanced, most of them including his mother thought that he is going to go to another institute and all of them advised "study well."

But the two years of his exposure in KISS and KITT had made him aware of the best institutes of the country and now his focus is to get admission into IIT Kharagpur. Nothing less than that. He knows that they have the best faculty and he would opt for mechanical branch. To that extent, he has clarity.

But the problem with him is that he cannot communicate well. In all personal interviews, he is unable to speak in English and lack in general knowledge, that becomes the first tool to impress many. He keeps saying to people that "I wish I was a better communicator and that would have given me more confidence to meet the students coming from all parts of our country." He feels that good communication would have helped him compete with any, since his domain knowledge is stronger. He always feels that he finds it difficult to choose the right word that impresses people, though he is confident that he would strive harder and pick up that skill too in IIT.

Funda is that domain knowledge of the subject is essential to succeed but never ignore good communication ability since it puts the icing on the cake that you win.

□

16

The seed of education in poor kids' mind gives best fruits

First story: His father was a laundryman. The 12-year-old boy eventually helped his father in door-to-door collection and delivery of clothes on a daily basis. And one of the houses in that delivery chain was the house of former Indian Cricketer, Arun Lal. It is well known to cricket fans that the gritty cricketer never scored a test century, but he and his wife, Debjani, played a great innings in humanity, particularly in the life of this laundry boy, which is little known to many.

The boy's acquaintance with Arun Lal and Debjani created a liking for sports in this boy. Since Arun Lal was staying in Kolkata, cricket could not impress this young mind but football that had a huge fan club in that city left a strong impression on him.

The young boy was with Young Bengal, a first-division football club. He wanted to become a professional footballer and would meet Arun Lal during training. The club was paying him around ₹ 10,000 per year along with food, which was too much for this young man. In fact, his association with Arun Lal also made him play u-16 cricket too.

It will not be really wrong if one says he had less interest in studies as his interest in sub-junior Bengal increased. But one day, Arun Lal said in a serious discussion with this boy that there were no guarantees in sports. That was a turning point. His interest in studies in his 9th standard grew and Debjani helped him with English, the tough subject then.

His life now was spent between two places – house of Arun Lal for studies, where he got his fresh orange juice free and the pavements of Bhavanipore, where his father had the laundry shop. The couple insisted that one hour of focussed study but daily makes a lot of difference for anyone's career. And that what exactly this young lad did, although the juice lured him to do so.

Thus, he later went on to do B.Com. and M.Com. Then he appeared for the CAT. In 2000, he got into IIM, Kolkata. This followed with jobs with Deutsche Bank and Credit Agricole followed, including a stint in London.

Then he went on to gift Lal's family with a Mercedes, while driving the relatively modest vehicles. He also helped them to move from an apartment into a bungalow. And the ultimate tribute, when that little boy, now 39, Bikash Chowdhary, got married to Kamna; the Chowdharys named their girl child as 'Arunima' after Arun.

Currently, Chowdhary is Associate Vice President at JSW Steel in Mumbai.

Second story: One of the weekend this year, my caretaker from my Nasik house called me up and said the mango from the trees in our house are aptly ripe and it is the time to enjoy the fruit. An impromptu party-like situation emerged at home and since the entire family was really busy through the weekend, I decided to drive down on Sunday morning to bring our first harvest from our own garden, although economically it is not the right way. Eventually, I spent more on petrol to get some five-dozen good fruits. But the organic fruit brought huge happiness among the entire family. Hence the "char anne ki murgi do rupaiye ka masala" dialogue was completely ignored. We all were waiting for such a result over the last three years since we planted these trees.

Yes, planting trees is important. They not only keep your environment clean, but also shower fruits. But sowing the seed of education in young minds probably yields a fruit of satisfaction that has no match for these perishable fruits.

Funda is that you must plant trees, but sow education seed in young minds, since the fruit of the latter is sweeter than the former.

□

17

Kindness and humanity are not (mathematically) measurable

Every summer month, most of the buildings in our entire suburbs buzz with activity, more particularly in the tennis court. The visiting relatives, friends and their children for a summer vacation generally play on the court more than the members of the society. In fact, some societies even charge an entrance fee per month for such relatives and the members grudgingly pay it as a children's play garden, elders park at the swimming pools, and tennis and squash courts are rarity in their villages.

This year, Shivaji Thodkar, a young man from Ratnagiri in Maharashtra and also a relative of one of our building residents came again and was seen seriously holding meetings with some retired members of the society.

I remember seeing him the last year in our building. What attracted me to this young lad was his ability to crack joke on himself at that young age, which clearly indicated that he was a happy soul, and also a fantastic tennis player, a game I love, though am not a great player.

He started enjoying the vacation in our colony and as it hit him that the exam results are on the corner, his happiness slowly started disappearing and, as a result, anxiety took its place.

Exam results are one such step towards our achievement. It affects our confidence. Most of us also worry about how others, especially family and close ones, might react to our results. A good exam result has become something to brag about to friends and relatives. A bad one is seen as the end of academic career.

I distinctly remember his words to one of our neighbors, wherein he said, "Uncle, it is a test of fire; passing or failing these exams makes we students feel positively or negatively about ourselves." Two days before the results, he withdrew from many activities, started moving alone everywhere, stopped smiling, despite we cracking jokes.

These words sent an alarm bell on some of us and we collectively decided not to leave this boy and other students alone whose exam results are expected soon. We approached a group of retired people in our colony and asked to take the responsibility. We also thought spending some money by taking them to a mall or a picture hall or a water park is worth enough. And we did so.

As feared, on the day of result, Todkar had a terrible time. He scored 62 percent in HSC exam, a percentage that has brought a heart-ache for his parents. It took three days for those seniors to convince his parents that the percentage is not bad as they think. Today, Todkar is in a reputed Pune college, doing brilliantly in his chosen subject.

The elders convinced him and his family with stories of Henry Ford, Bill Gates, Walt Disney, Albert Einstein, Thomas Edison, and Sachin Tendulkar – who had a real tough time with their academics, yet made it successful with their determination and belief in their own abilities.

This year Todkar is back in the colony, requesting some of our retired residents to accompany him for a week as his guest at his place, so that no village student takes any extreme step before and after the results. Yesterday

I saw those colony elders, who were beaming with joy and expressed how they are taking turns and making a difference in that village for youths. I did not dare ask them to quantify their act since I know humanity cannot be mathematically calculated.

Funda is that humanity and kindness are not measurable since it is not business; they just need to be felt and realized.

□

18

Parenting is an institution, please nurture it

Parent 1: May is the month when most parents in my friend-circle post their children's graduation or post-graduation ceremonies either in Dallas, or Stanford or California or Manchester or at London School of Economics in our WhatsApp group. Amidst these deluge of 'success stories' one story attracted my attention; the story of Rahil, who is just 15 years old and stays in Indore. He studies in one of the best colleges locally, Daly College. Not an academically inclined student by "Indian standard" (since we perceive that only 90 percent and above are academically inclined), but, at the same time not an average student as well. Until 6th standard, he was really a bright student. Post 7th, his attention got into sports—played squash at national and international levels but had a huge crush with soccer, Manchester United being the most favourite soccer team, and spent most of his time watching football in this cricketing nation. That kept his academic score between 65 and 70 percent in all higher classes and he expects the same score in the 10th exam, whose results are yet to come.

One morning, his mother, a home-maker, Arpana Saboo posted in one of the WhatsApp group: "My 15-year-old son finally got an admission into the Liverpool Academy and I had faith that it would happen."

Apparently, on day before night this week, he got a call from Liverpool International Academy for a one-year residential soccer coaching class at Pune and this year, he will be playing soccer instead of putting academics on the front seat. He may appear for 11th or may not.

In an era where every parent is posting the children's academic excellence in social networking platform, Arpana was certainly different. She said, "As parents, we don't want to deny him something that he is so passionate about; one can catch up with education even later in life." And believe me, it is a bold statement in this era.

Parent 2: Son of a vendor at the village market in Moynaguri, Kolkata, Sanjay Sarkar watched his father skip meals to pay for his tuitions. He decided to shift to his aunt's place since it is closer to his school, so that he could save on travel expenses and live on mid-day meals he gets there. After his school hours, Sanjay doubled his daily study time to eight hours, since the picture of his father skipping meal was replayed in his mind always. And this week, his back-breaking hard work and sacrifices of his family were rewarded. The 18-year-old ranked second in the Higher Secondary merit list, a no-mean feat for someone who had to battle odds throughout his student life.

Parent 3: This 9-year-old hasn't been home for the last two years for a vacation or festival and lives and studies at an ashram at Nashik. Three years ago, his father, at Jalgaon, Maharashtra, committed suicide after he failed to meet the growing need of his children and also repay a loan. His mother ended her life too. And there are many like him there, devastated and vulnerable by the death of their parents.

Parents and children today often complain that they do not understand each other. That is basically because all parents compare their children with their peers and children are unaware of the parents struggle behind bringing them up. And this widens the gap, say experts, who suggest parents to avoid falling in this trap and create healthy parent-child relationship at home.

Funda is that adults' attitude towards children needs to shift and there is no best or worst parenting, since it is an institution it needs to evolve on its own as per needs. But nurturing it is in our hands.

□

19

Some unknown successes end up teaching the life's best lessons

Well-known Success: This week, the whole country got elated when a 21-year-old New Delhi girl Tina Dabi topped the civil services examination (CSE) 2015, that too in her very first attempt. The second position as per CSE results was bagged by J&K domicile candidate, Athar Aamir ul Safi Khan, while Delhi's Jasmeet Singh Sandhu stood third in the competitive exam for appointment to elite government services, such as the IAS, IPS and IFS. Tina, probably one of the youngest civil services toppers, is the second Delhi girl to top the exam in consecutive years after Ira Trivedi achieved the feat last year.

Little-known Success: A 29-year-old grocer's daughter from West Bengal, who takes pride in saying how her parents gave her the best of education despite battling abject poverty, has stood 19th in the civil services exam, realising her dream of becoming an IAS officer. Sweta Agarwal had qualified for IPS last year and was training at the National Police Academy, Hyderabad, when she got this news. It was a day of double delight and a dilemma. Her rank is the highest attained by any Bengal candidate in years.

Despite going through abject poverty, they sent her to the best schools possible. Sweta went to St Joseph's School, Auxilium Convent and St Xavier's College, all in Kolkata, where she was first-class first in the entire university. Her parents went to Hindi-medium schools, but made sure she knew English. And she will be the first IAS officer from her locality. Her parents, despite being a baniya had never thought of marrying her off their only child.

Unknown successes: On the first Sunday of every month, children staying in Basavanagar's Tata Sherwood Apartments at Bengaluru collect old newspapers from all 400-odd houses. This idea may not be new to many. Even these newspaper heaps that are sold and converted into money cannot be new. But what is new is that the amount is spent on the children of 150-odd maids, drivers and helps, who work in the colony for their school fees and for buying their books and periodicals. This indirectly has reduced the school dropouts to zero.

This idea was initiated three years before. But what they saw was poor performance of these children. So, again the group has stepped in and, now, volunteers from the apartment complex are conducting daily classes to help them build a bright future.

The program is called SEE and eight volunteers from different backgrounds of IT, HR and marketing teach students from classes 6 to 10.

The idea to start such work began in 2014, when a cook working in one of the houses collapsed and needed a surgery that was costing around ₹ 5 lakhs. The residents raised the amount in 96 hours but fortunately the hospital also gave a discount later knowing their intentions, which helped them save a considerable amount. Instead of distributing the money back to each member, they decided to embark on this plan and keep the project alive. They came up with an idea of old newspapers' sale.

Last year in July, the residents decided to conduct classes in the TATA Sherwood clubhouse for two hours on Sundays. That slowly became regular classes with volunteers teaching English and Mathematics to all, which now has grown to Science and Social Sciences. The result this year is 'no fail'. For them, no failure in that 'help' community is like making their children achieve 90 percent.

Funda is that every success is superb. But some unknown successes, like this, teach some fantastic lessons.

□

20

Organising blue-collar job facility is the next big business

Javed Akhtar dropped out of school at 7th standard. The monetary pressure at home resulting into tense environment made him look for a job that could support his mother that had a direct impact on physical abuse of his father on his mother.

He got into electrician and plumbing job, which had sporadic earning but that was enough to handle the situation then. Over the years, Javed despite being good at work, his earnings could even meet the expenses that he incurred in on his motorcycle, that he recently brought with the help of private moneylender. In fact, he was slowly getting into the same shoes of his father, with lesser money, more commitment, married life, children needs and the pressure for money slowly eating away the peace at home.

Dinesh Goel, Gaurav Toshniwal, and Kunal Jadhav, all IIT alumnii from Mumbai, know not one such Javed but several of them whose income is sporadic, low but good at their work.

So, they founded a company in November 2014 called 'Aasaanjobs', where today more than 150 people are employed and over 180,000 people like Javed are enrolled, whose services are offered to over 3,000 companies.

In fact, this market has more niche companies, like 'Easyfix', 'Timesaverz', 'one-time jobs' among others, who not only appoints Javed-like caliber employees, but a connects common man, who wants also reliable service.

People like Javed, when they sign up with such companies, undergo multiple sessions of skilling and training at these startups and today in a span of two years, and people like Javed are finding better job prospects and increase in revenues. These companies not only embark upon soft skills but also upgrade them up-to-date technical knowledge that can match customer expectations, training the workforce in newer technologies, thus bringing professionalism and quality of service which has become deciding factors for these startups.

On the other hand, Javed and his friends who signed up early had become the area supervisors in these companies, who now have stable income and, more particularly and, peace at home, Javed having an ability to zoom away in his favourite motorcycle whenever he wants. Javed today is making anything between ₹ 30,000 and ₹ 40,000, depending upon the overtime.

Starting from on-field training to classroom training, including telephone training is something that these companies are concentrating upon to provide 24/7 reliable services.

The first thing these companies concentrated on was the tools that they use. They do not allow any 'Jugad' in the areas of plumbing and electrical fittings. They charge a bit more but all materials used and process adopted are as professional as it happens in foreign countries, thus bringing a lot of "wow" factor to this unorganised sector, which was mostly between the plumber and electricians with their customers.

Background verification is something these companies insist on as each of their blue-collared employees are entering the high-end homes and companies.

'Aasaanjobs' has managed to enter smaller towns and Mumbai suburbs without opening an office there. They list out the services provided; they enroll skilled people from a particular area; train them and link them to customers when they require their services. Dinesh Goel is confident of getting into cities without any physical infrastructure and by using iCloud as the tool to bring blue-collared employees and customers face-to-face.

'Aasaanjobs' is getting popular among the blue-collar job-seekers primarily because there is no online recruitment firm specifically serving their need, which currently serves Mumbai, Pune and NCR areas, leaving the whole country wide open to other competitors who may contemplate to start similar services to deal with low-end jobs.

Funda is that menial work is a wide market and completely unorganised across the country and organising them is a big business by itself.

□

21

Just keep the fire on, nothing is impossible

She was eight-year-old, staying just opposite to Chandrapur railway station in east Maharashtra and a daughter of a Rickshawala's driver, and her pastime was playing on the railway track, bogies standing on the shunting line and hiding and running around all the railway properties to play her favourite game of hide-and-seek with her siblings and peers. When her mother yells from her house "Jyotsna, come and have your food", she could hear it clearly and she would run to eat.

In 1995 summer, her mother called up in the same way when she was playing inside a train. Since she did not answer, she told herself, 'Let her come today. I will break her leg for not listing to me and playing all through the day in the train', and got back to her kitchen chores. Little did she know that her eight-year-old daughter was sleeping in one of the top berths of the train and it moved already. The girl, when she woke up, did not realise that she has been sleeping for over 16 hours. All her attempts to stop the train went in vain and the co-passengers only took pity on her but none came forward to help.

After a 20-hour long journey, the little girl was in Mumbai. She went to the helpful strangers, asking for a train that would take her back to Chandrapur. Someone pointed out one. It was a wrong train or she heard it wrong, but this time she de-boarded and she was in Secunderabad. It had been over a day since she had a meal and her mother's call but she was nowhere closer to her home. She begged for help and kept repeating Chandrapur and nobody seemed to have heard that name there.

She went to an eatery for food. The owner promised to arrange for her return journey but made her a domestic help at his place. A year later, during a southern trip, when she was unwell, the family threw her out. And she was back on the railway station and asking strangers to help her reach Chandrapur.

This time, the train took her to Bengaluru where the railway police spotted and admitted her to a children's home. Her life from here on was a blur of entries and exits. Though she went to school, she was kicked out of one hostel to another but learnt several skills run by these hostels.

A hostel arranged her marriage with a screen painting artist, M. Shivashakti and the couple had a daughter and son in the next five years. Since she learnt computers and also knew Kannada, and spoken but broken English, she got a job of a receptionist at a software company.

But her hunt for Chandrapur and parents continued. One of her colleagues helped her get in touch with Chandrapur police station and a woman constable took her complaint. The Chandrapur district S.P., Sandip Diwan took interest in this case, when it was brought before him, and ordered to dug up all two-decade-old files. Two weeks before, the police found the missing complaint of an auto-rickshaw driver Namdev and the police tracked him down in the city and confirmed the incident. One of the weekend this year, the family got an emotional reunion after 21 years, where parents always presumed that Jyotsna was dead. Now she is planning to take her parents and siblings to Bengaluru for future prospects.

Funda is that nothing is impossible for anyone if you keep that fire to accomplish burning all through.

□

22

Your hobbies can connect you globally

The 32-year-old Vijay Aarvamudhan is an auditor from Axis Bank and he commutes to his home everyday in Mumbai city by local train. Everyday, for at least 30 minutes to one hour, he gets down anywhere in the network and waits there for some time. He is not alone. There are 150 professionals working in various organisations doing like this.

If you see them waiting in the railway station platforms, you will see no difference between the normal passengers and them. They will be doing everything a passenger does. Reading newspapers, buying some eatables from the vendors, often looking at the watch as if waiting for a particular train, asking questions with fellow passengers, answering patiently the questions asked by any new-comers to that station among many. One difference an observant can spot is that they are always noting down something in their small diary or in the lap/palm-top.

And the major difference between them and the normal passenger is that when the train arrives in the platform, they do not board the train but watch others boarding the train. They take every detail of the boarding process. From bogie number, train number, number of people boarding that train and in each compartment, the way they are boarding, the luggage they are carrying among many other things, they note carefully.

Then the noted contents are carefully compared each hour with other hours of the day; each Monday with other 51 Mondays of the year; each week of that year; every year with the previous years and decade and many more interesting comparisons. The outcome is that there are interesting and curious generating information that Indian Railways themselves seek from these people and they happily share with them.

Meet the members of Indian Railways Fan Club, an association of rail enthusiasts connected by an electronic discussion forum called IRFCA members and spread over not only across the country, but globally.

The global members of this hobby group are over 8,000 and 150 are from the city like Mumbai, where the train services are more of a lifeline.

Their notes help any railways across the globe to get into finer details of their operation and this fan club has pioneered several initiatives for good.

People like Vijay, who has passion for trains, sit down in different stations and note down every detail possible. If someone speaks to them, you will mistake them for some very senior railway board officials. To that extent, their findings are exhaustive. Whenever the zonal railway officials needed to have some in-depth study or pattern, they seeked help from these volunteers, whose hobby is observing train services.

In fact, the repair yard gets exact details of torn seats, non-working fans, broken latches and switches and many more details from these people and yard people always get in touch with these members instead of looking for faults in the bogies during servicing.

They do global interaction, compare with other cities of the world and suggest the railway authorities how to handle a particular issue. Apart from that, these members are the first one to come to know about any new initiatives taken by any railway authorities in the world since the members share those info in their WhatsApp group. They even suggest interior and exterior colours that can withstand rough weather and usage, based in other global railways' experience, besides giving a soothing feeling to the passengers. Each city's passengers' behaviour is observed by them.

Funda is that a simple activity like rail enthusiasts' hobby not only benefits regular travellers, but it also creates huge purpose for a giant organisation like railways and connects you globally.

□

23

Make children understand the difference between prestige and false prestige

"Sir, you seem to be educated. Can you help me get my son back home? I have enough land to get food for at least the next two generations, but he is not understanding me," the man in his 40s was pleading with me on one of my stops during my long weekend drive in Maharashtra.

When I asked him to elaborate, he said that he got his son admitted to the nearby engineering college because some of his friends were doing so. He did not do well in studies. But for the last few weeks, he stopped coming home, and so many other children from that Yeowla village near Nasik. The detergent manufacturing company they claim to have been working for has provided them all expenses paid salaried job and this old man was suspecting how one can pay without getting anything in return.

Curiosity led me to that place. And I heard some motivator speaking:

"I have no doubt in my mind that you all understand far better than many outside this place that with what difficulty our parents educate us; am sure you also understand this fact that when they send that money for our education and they sleep half stomach, but with a smile and hope that one day their son will earn some money and would wipe my tears." "Am I right or wrong?" asked not a very matured voice, which came out from that room.

Quickly the reply came in chorus: Yes, we understand.

This enthusiasm and the motivational words stopped me going inside and the voice continued:

"Now if you go back and work on your father's field, what your *gaon wala* will think about you? With what face will your parents walk in that village you come from? Will you and your family have any pride? And, finally, who will respect you, who will give you a girl to marry?" Many unanswered questions were being shot at.

I peeped in from that broken window. The young sad faces nodded in unison and the speaker on their behalf asked "*No na*?" And they all nodded in affirmative.

Then the young speaker continued, "At least, if you earn ₹ 5,000 per month with food and accommodation taken care of, those great souls, I mean your parents, will sleep peacefully that their son is managing his own life."

All those young faces lit like Deepavali lamps with hope and aspiration.

Taking advantage of that momentary happiness in those young faces, the speaker promised a career that will change their fortune once they worked hard.

I allowed my eyes to scan that low middle-class house. It had several bunker beds, at least 17 of them, which means all 50 people were staying there and with one toilet to serve them. The house looked to me as if a villager wearing the most fashionable French dress in uncomfortableness.

The room had some modern electronic gadgets that are certainly not essential to any village life. And those silly items, like tea kettle, mobile battery bank, steam iron among others are apparently being shown the most essential of modern life.

Later, in the night, when I met some of them in their parents' presence, I could realise that how much these young minds have been brainwashed towards false prestige and their parents' perception. The parents were ready to embrace their children the way they are while the children were dreaming of a life, far away from reality.

Funda is that save your children from being brainwashed by outsiders, who always make the false prestige as real prestige of life. It is sad but true.

□

24

Change yourself than waiting for the situation to change

Rahul was always irregular to his classes. But his way impressing girls, particularly Anupama, the most beautiful girl in the class, was through his sport. For him living, breathing, eating, sleeping and attending classes start with cricket and end with cricket period.

That is the reason when he came to the class with gloves on and started writing notes with it for hours, they were feeling odd and started gossiping about him.

Everyone in the class was giggling like we all did in our school seeing something funny. The whispering talk amidst all students for that one hour was "stupid idea of wearing the gloves and writing to show off that he plays cricket". What added fuel to the gossip was his failure to impress with his individual score in the recently concluded two Ranji trophy matches.

After the class, he came out and approached his friend Adarsh to borrow his accounts notes since the examination was hanging over his head. Rahul promised to return those notes after photocopying the relevant pages.

While handing over the notes, Adarsh quickly replied "Rahul, tell me why were you wearing gloves on all through the class? You came to the class wearing gloves and continued wearing them even when the teacher was dictating notes! Is it to impress Anupama?

Rahul quickly jumped to his own defence and said, "No...no, she is already impressed, I don't have to impress her anymore." But Adarsh and Rajdeep were persistent to get answer to that madness.

Then Rahul started in a polite manner and explained his stand for wearing cricket gloves in the class. Rahul's face was a bit-low lit when he said, "You know something Adarsh, in the last two Ranji matches which I played, I had the old gloves and the old gloves were very loose. Since the gloves were loose, when the bowler bowled, the ball just went past my gloves and it created a small snick sound. The wicket keeper caught it, he appealed and both the times even though my bat didn't touch the ball, I was given caught behind."

"Then I told myself that enough is enough, this can't continue and I bought these gloves and I wanted my hands get accustomed to wearing these new gloves and sweat as much as it can. So, for the next 48 hours, I will wear these gloves continuously because the next Ranji match, which is a semifinal, is in two days. I want my hands to get adjusted to there pair of gloves. I am not going to remove the gloves even when I am sleeping, even when I am eating, even when I am coming to class because I want to do well in the next match and I want my hands to be comfortable in them."

Some friends who understood cricket praised for his thought, while those who did not understand the game well, went back to their respective classes, saying, "Style marta hai."

In the ensuing Ranji semifinals against Saurashtra, he scored a century. In the finals, Karnataka played against Delhi that year. He scored another century and, based on those two performances, he got selected for the Indian cricket team, which went to England, and surprisingly in the first test match in England, he scored 90-odd runs.

He took the responsibility for his life. He had a very strong internal focus and control and did not blame the external circumstances, like the umpiring decisions. He decided to change himself and do his best. And that Rahul was none other than Dravid.

Funda is that if you change yourself and go ahead without waiting for the situation to change, the chances of winning are far better.

□

25

Success in studies and life is not really connected to each other

I am very depressed since the last three days with newspapers from Ahmedabad to Bhubaneswar, carrying at least one depressing news about some final-year school children taking off their lives because they failed in some mock examinations conducted just before the board examination as a matter of practice.

And the news items finally concluded that there is a mismatch between their ability to study and the parents' expectations from the board exam results.

But there was one set of parents who did not care how their son was performing. Their son also had no or little interest in his studies. As it is, his father was struggling to keep jobs and the lower-income family had bad news from the school front too. Finally, the boy got dropped out at the age of 15 and got a job as a janitor (Jamadhar) just to help support the family.

He used to crack jokes, made most of his jokes from his failures and people laughed at it because the joke was not at them. Since he made many laugh, and did not do well in studies, many thought he will be play some 'stupid' role in some drama or some street play.

Since 1980s, comic stand-up shows in USA and Canada were famous like our TV laughter shows with people like Kapil Sharma and others alike happening nowadays in India. He went for his first audition by borrowing money to Canada.

On his first comic stand-up at a club in Toronto, he was booed off-stage. Later, when he auditioned for a TV programme called Saturday Night in 1980, he failed to land the part.

Then he did another stupid thing. He wrote a cheque for himself for a sum of $10,000,000 million (₹ 680,000,000) and behind the cheque, he wrote the cheque is paid to him "for the acting services rendered" and kept it in his purse.

People closer to him thought he is as usual a mad guy. Like some of us remove those crispy ₹ 1,000 notes and keep counting them sometimes despite the fact we know that it is not going to add more notes, he took out that cheque and kept seeing it everyday, literally everyday for seven years, until one day he received a cheque exactly for the same amount which was paid "for acting services he rendered" for a movie called Dumb and Dumber.

Most of us in India know him as the "The Mask Man". And his name is Jim Carey, laugh-out-loud zany comic guy, who's brought us some of the highest-grossing comedies of all time.

Closer home, there is one person. You may not know him. He was also not good at Maths and Chemistry. He cleared his PU course after five attempts. And by the time he did it, his classmates had already completed their engineering course. But his story had just begun. Wherever he went, he was told he is too old to start at the place he applied. He felt insulted and crumbled within but did not lose hope.

Kiran Jonnalagadda now features in the team that developed the Human Protein Reference Database by Johns Hopkins University. The database contains entries on the 3,000 most-studied human proteins and their roles in diseases and is supposed to be the standard of developing a database internationally. Kiran has come a long way from an unsuccessful PU candidate to a successful entrepreneur.

Funda is that pressurising the children to excel in studies is fine only to an extent since success in studies and life is not really interlinked, at least in some cases I know.

□

26
Everyone is a hero

First story: Last night, I sat down on my office computer to train a new sub editor Ritesh Shukla in our office about how to write a story. Next four minutes when I typed the copy, there was a silence around. Many eyes were looking at me on my ability to type stories flawlessly.

Fortunately, I typed the story without a single mistake and raised from the seat with a pride and for a second, one man crossed my mind. Behram contractor, one of the great journalists I worked with, had the habit of giving his copy without a single mistake on his sheets when news were typed in a typewriter, which had no auto spell-correction facility.

Today, he is not there in this world and his wife Farzana runs his afternoon paper started by him. He was very keen to teach this practice to all we young journalists then with grit and I was always determined that I should become like him someday, writing flawless copy and when I do that on my daily routine, which is very rare, he always crosses my mind at least for a fraction of a second. He has been my hero as far as clean copy is concerned.

Second story: He is from a small town called Pali in Rajasthan. If one wants to crack joke on him, one can easily say that he is an expert in failing.

He failed twice in 12th; four times in first-year

graduation; and almost in every competitive exam he wrote, taking the total of failed attempts to 19. He made an attempt to appear from pre-medical test to basic school-teaching certificate test. Passing the examination kept eluding him.

Every time he appeared for the exam, the past fear of failure never chased him. He always hoped to clear the exam, but did not succeed. This record holder in failing exams was too disappointed like any other children of these days, but did not take any extreme steps like some of the children across the country are taking.

His friends became his inspiration. They kept him encouraging to reappear and try hard. And they never allowed him to get disappointed.

His heroes were his friends who managed to crack the IAS exams. He also felt cracking them but never allowed his previous failures to create shadow in his grit and hope. So, he studied hard and made attempts there too but failed there too. He wanted to reappear but unfortunately crossed his age-limit that barred him to appear again for IAS exam.

Not losing heart he went ahead and appeared for Rajasthan Administrative Services (RAS) and got passed out and also got a job in the state government office.

Meet Dalpat Singh, who is posted as an officer in Public Health Engineering Department at Udaipur's local government office.

Today, most media, encourage the students across the country who are taking extreme steps just in a fear of failing examination, are carrying his story of failures. And Dalpat Singh is speaking about it openly, although many of us always like to conceal our failures, so that his failed stories can save at least a few lives, if not all, being sniffed out at an early age.

Everyone must identify that grit, that passion, that

determination and sail through the life which has thrones along with a bed of roses.

Funda is that success and failures are not the story; it is grit to do something and succeed is the story. And that grit actually makes you a hero to someone knowingly or unknowingly.

□

27

Life always offers tangibles and intangibles; few choose the latter

He is a Maths teacher for the last 23 years. But his life's balance sheet in all these years never grew in mathematical terms, I mean profit. Because Maths is all about tangible things, clear profit, numbers and so on, which is not his concern.

He improved the standard of living of most of his students by educating them, making them understand Maths, number, money and, finally, all tangible things. They all grew up to become successful men and women, some moved to Gulf while some moved within the state of Kerala and everyone grew in their materialistic life.

But he decided to keep his life's standard at the level he started at 1993. Because it had no or few materials and pots and pots of happiness, the most intangible thing of life, only those who possessed can understand and enjoy.

It was not an easy life then. Having lost his father at an early age, with elder brother gone to Gulf for job in order to support family, he took the responsibility of supporting six more siblings below him.

Everyone suggested teacher's job is the most stable one and he managed to get one in a primary school by paying ₹ 50,000 which was sent by his brother.

He got the job too. Then he realised that it is a tough one. The school in which he got the job was less than three kms away from his house. But it took six hours of the day in both directions.

Abdul Malik was born, brought up and studied in the Koodalangadi panchayat in Malappuram in Kerala and he didn't have to cross the Kadalundi river till he got a job to teach Maths in Padinajattumuri in the same panchayat.

Three hours of bus travel, changing two buses to reach his workplace took a toll on his happiness quotient. He could not leave the job because he paid a huge amount to get it.

One day, while returning from school, he saw a person swimming across the river to get banana from the farm, that is situated next to his house on the other side of the river. Next day that stranger volunteered to return along with him. Wow, that changed his life! He took exactly 24 minutes to return home against three hours of bus travel, that too without spending a penny. It was 1993.

For the last 23 years, he goes to work in the same fashion. Abdul Malik, a Maths teacher at the Muslim Lower Primary School in Malappuram, Kerala, hit the headlines when photographs of his swimming to school everyday appeared in the newspapers, including the BBC recently.

At the river bank, he changes into a towel that he carries in a plastic bag. He then gets into the water with a tube around his chest.

His lunch box, sandals, plastic bag and an umbrella are all clutched in one hand that he keeps raised above the water.

On the other bank, he has identified a rock behind where he dresses to go to school. He keeps the tube tied to a small rock.

Other than teaching Maths, Malik tries to do away with the fear some children have of the water by teaching them swimming in the summer, when the river is less turbulent.

He is not aware of how successful his students are in life, but he is confident that he has taught them not to destroy or pollute the natural resources and has created a generation in the last two decades that live and protect nature.

Today, for Malik, it is a different Mathematics of deriving happiness from nature than just accumulating materialistic possessions.

Funda is that life offers many opportunities. Those who pay off attention to intangibles lead a great life than those who choose tangibles.

□

28

The 'hero' post in every city, suburb and neighbourhood is vacant; grab it!

First story: In 2004, it was a summer holiday. This 10th class, New Delhi student, having finished his exam earlier than many, decided to visit the neighbourhood Thyagraja stadium.

There he saw some foreigners playing a game, which looked similar to the football game they played, yet it was completely different, including the ball.

Intrigued about this game, he stayed there the whole evening to know every side of the game called Rugby, played all over the world fondly. Later, he saw this game on television too.

Then he was regular, understood the nuances of the game and went back to his place, which is a small urban village called 'Maidangarhi' situated in the congested lane of South Delhi and started teaching the game to his fellow schoolmates, who later became collegemates too.

His enthusiasm caught like a wild fire among the youngsters and today this particular place has sent lots of players to the national level. As in today in the world of rugby, this small urban village is known as "rugby capital of India".

Meet Indian rugby team captain, Gautam Nagar, and Deepak Nagar, who represented India in 2010 Delhi

Commonwealth Games and the subsequent Asian Games held in China.

Maidengarhi's date with rugby started in 2004 and these duo brought in a title for their place in flat 6 years.

Second story: If you ask about a suburb near Mumbai called Mumbra, people will look at you suspiciously since this place is known for lots of crimes and illegal activities than anything major that one recalls fast.

In that suburb, you visit today, almost all auto-rickshaws would carry a small poster about their hero, egg- and meat-selling shops will have his poster and every gymnasium will certainly have its local hero picture.

At least over 100 drug addicts have kicked off their bad habits and turned into making their health as their wealth, thanks to the inspiration given by a 28-year-old local hero.

This 5.9-ft physique hero has lost his father at 12 and a college dropout. Being a Salman Khan fan, he decided to make his body like him. That decision followed his countless hours in gym, and early this month, he won the first position in the super tall category at the contest held in Amateur Bodybuilders' Association of Maharashtra. Meet Manaoor A Mukadam, who particiapted in "Mr. India" crown at the national championship held in Mengaluru.

Irrespective of his winning, he has at least changed the life of many youngsters, who have slightly slipped away from leading healthy life to drugged life. And today when Mukadam walks on the potholed, crowded and filth-filled Mumbra roads, he cannot avoid strangers staring at him because he is their local hero.

Third story: Car pooling and odd-even car scheme is alien for Jharkhand but that doesn't mean they can't think green.

Even before other cities have thought of any collective green effects, all above 45-year-old successful professionals from Ranchi like Sanjay Kumar Singh from Indian Institute of Coal Management, A.K. Singh, director of voluntary outfit and CCL Sports manager, Adil Hussain, under whose captaincy once Indian one-day captain M.S. Dhoni played, all switched to cycle to save environment.

They pedal at least six to 12 kms everyday to work and to do errands. They are the local heroes for many.

Funda is that the post of hero is always vacant and evolving in every small community and neighbourhood. Grab it by doing something different.

□

29

Exposure is the only tool that will make the future generation brighter

The 15-year-old, Vijay Chauhan, is not the young character of the role played by Amitabh Bachchan in the film Agnipath. Vijay Chauhan is just like other hundreds of youngsters who was born in the house of a landless daily wage worker in one of the remote villages in Bihar.

He migrated to Punjab at that young age of 15 for a job and got it too. He realised that the petty salary he received was not enough to support even his basic necessities. Hence, he decided to go back and continue his studies.

That is when he came in contact with "Professionals' Alliance for Youth's Growth", also called PRAYOG, is the brain-child of Surya Prakash Rai, started in one of the remote villages situated in Gopalganj district of Bihar.

PRAYOG is a platform which is catering to the needs of children from lesser advantaged communities by filling the deficit of infrastructure, health and education facilities in villages. Started in one village currently, PRAYOG is serving more than 600 kids of 12 villages at present, realising that the best way to reach out to the kids was by offering them something which they had never experienced before. Hence, PRAYOG library was set up in a community open space in June 2013. The first day saw a mere five students walking in haltingly, but within a year's time, the library was a hit and saw a regular footfall of hundreds of students.

The books covered a vast range. From newspapers to weekly and monthly magazines, the books were offered to the students according to their choice. Another initiative that helped Surya in grabbing people's attention was exposure visits. First he took only five kids, where they learnt yoga, dancing and painting. Though the trip was not anything extraordinary, it gave a huge boost to the kids' confidence.

The second exposure trip was organised with 15 students to Bhutan, which again was a big success. In the second trip only, students who picked up all-round development were picked up, which indirectly sent a message to all other children the advantage of being smart and aware.

The kids were asked to write on a topic – "How to create a model village" and asked them to ideate. Thus, they were made to participate in the general welfare of the village development.

Surya identified two major problems—education and electricity. Since most of the villagers were illiterate, they did not consider their children's education as their priority.

Apart from lack of awareness, a low teacher-student ratio was another challenge. Kids were more willing to attend tuition classes than school. There was a serious lack of interest from parents' and students' side and the global awareness slowly changed by infusing competition in them.

To solve electricity issue wherein the student is not able to study after sunset, the PRAYOG team gave away solar lamps to all students who won some competition like easy competition of others. This gave them a competitive spirit.

A basic solar study lamp costs ₹ 450 and the entire project of giving lamp to all students needed ₹ 90,000 to become operational.

PRAYOG has a tie-up with Prajnopaya Foundation, a Massachusetts Institute of Technology initiative, wherein both the organisations will be supporting 'Global Literacy Project', whereby 100 children between 3 and 8 years of age would be supported with technology.

Funda is that basic exposure to kids is enough to make them brighter than they are. We have been saying in this column that the kids of this generation are brighter than we were in those days. What they need is a small help to show the path. They will run faster than we expect.

□

30

Fortune always favours the brave

He was born blind. He was born in a poor family. His parents were living in a village, where inclusion of challenged people was never heard of. His society believed in sin one did in the past life and, hence, had a mindset to accept all bad things happening to them was due to 'karma', which means they never tried to fight it out.

When he was growing up, his father, a farmer, would take him to the fields but the little boy couldn't be of any help. His father then decided that he might as well study.

Like any other village boy story, he also went to a school which was five kms away from his village. But when he went to school, he was pushed to the back-benches. Even teachers did not like students who cannot see them and respond to their teaching. And other students obviously did not include him in PT classes or at play.

Realising that the son has learnt nothing, the father managed to save some money and sent him to a special school in Hyderabad.

The compassion, love and attention that he got in that school changed his outlook. He not only started understanding the subjects but he excelled in them. The attention changed everything.

He played chess and cricket and excelled in them. He topped his class, even embracing an opportunity to work with late President Dr. A.P.J. Abdul Kalam in the Lead India project.

But none of this mattered much because he was denied admission to the science stream in class XI.

He cleared the Andhra Pradesh class X state board exams with over 90 percent marks, but the board said he could only take Arts subjects after that.

He sued the government and fought for six months. In the end, he got a government order that said he could take the science subjects but at his 'own risk'.

He got all the textbooks converted to audio books, worked day and night to complete XII board exams at 98 percent.

Then the similar refusal from IIT and BITS, Pilani came to him. He did not lose heart. He applied to schools in the US and got into the top four – MIT, Stanford, Berkeley, and Carnegie Mellon.

He went to MIT (with a scholarship) as the first international blind student in that school's history.

Towards the end of his bachelor's course in his mind, the 'what next' question came up, it brought him back to where he had started from. Questions that bothered him included: Why should a disabled child be pushed to the back row in the class? Why should the 10 percent of the disabled population of India be left out of the Indian economy? Why can't they make a living like everyone else with dignity?

He came to India to start an enterprise. Meet Srikanth Bolla, the CEO of Hyderabad-based Bollant Industries, an organisation that employs uneducated disabled employees to manufacture eco-friendly, disposable consumer packaging solutions, which is worth ₹ 50 crores.

Today, Srikanth has four production plants, one each in Hubli (Karnataka) and Nizamabad (Telangana), and two in Hyderabad (Telangana). Another plant, which will be 100 percent solar-energy operated, is coming up in Sri City, an integrated business city of AP.

His company's co-founder is Swarnalata, his anchor, support and special needs' teacher all through his life, who now trains all the 70 percent disabled employees at Bollant.

Funda is that if you want to be rich and change your fortune, then you need to cross the threshold limits set by your society boldly.

□

31

Only involvement and not education always takes you to life's high

Same old sad story we all are used to. Father was a drunkard. Mother is a maid. In meagre income the mother tried to educate all four children—two girls and two boys. Though financial crisis was the order of the day, one fine day, the crisis hit super low. The option before the mother was to take one of the children out from school and give her the responsibility of managing the house so that she can work in more houses.

Rukmini was the third child but the axe fell on her, the first-standard girl, because the elder sister was polio-affected. So, at the age of seven, with a tag called "first-standard dropped-out", V.P. Rukmini started shouldering the family responsibility.

She learnt to cook and clean the house before her family returned. After years of such struggle, she was married to an uneducated man who works in a store. It was marriage that brought her to Bengaluru in 1998 and she started working in a garment factory, Texport Overseas Group Company.

She joined a social organisation that worked for garment workers and from 2004 to 2006, she worked as a convenor. To support garment workers legally, she became the general secretary of a labour union and served it in that capacity from 2006 to 2011.

With immense experience, Rukmini became an expert to handle counselling, health issues, unionisation, women's and labour rights, labour laws, laws related to garment employees state insurance, provident fund and leadership and organisational management skills and along with like-minded garment workers, Rukmini established Garment Labour Union (GLU) in 2012 and she is present since then.

She did not stop there. She was constantly thinking how to solve and bring out the humiliation suffered by garment workers in public so that at least some of their problems gets solved. She herself was the victim of several abuses and humiliation from the hands of supervisors and bosses when she was a simple worker.

She wanted to raise her voice against all types of injustice against the garment workers. Her in-depth knowledge on subjects like from the use of new technology, to developing textile standards and the need for fair trade, from the merits and perils of unionisation to understanding labour laws, from occupational health hazards to career progression, from recycling cloth waste to meetings with micro-entrepreneurs, from issues of sexual harassment to the need for social security, attracted everyone.

At least 85 percent of the women workers out of six lakh garment workers working in over 1,200 garment factories in Bengaluru believed in Rukmini since she was fighting 24/7 for their welfare.

Today, she lends her voice to the silently suffering garment workers through her radio series program called 'Behind the Label'.

The series, produced by garment workers, attempts to tell stories of people who make our clothes. Started in June this year on a community radio, the series is being heard from Monday to Friday between 8 a.m. and 8:30 a.m. with a repeat in the evening from 6 p.m. to 6:30 p.m.

and it relays some of the best heart-warming stories of struggle and victory. So far, 80 stories have been on air.

Rukmini collects stories either at factories or at the houses of workers. She brings voice clips to the studio and edits and produces her own shows. For a first-standard drop-out to become the voice of hundreds of distressed workers is quite an achievement.

Funda is that if a first-standard drop-out has a mission to change the lives of over six lakh workforce in one area of industrialisation with her zeal and involvement, then all we educated can do wonders.

□

32

More experience helps you choose better things in life

First person: I saw 26-year-old Remmi Mathew from France promoting heritage walk organised by the Udaipur Municipal Corporation in association with a private company in front of the Jagannatha temple at Udaipur.

It was not his tall body, handsome look and his fair completion that made him different, but his readiness to do any work made him stand out in that foreigner visiting the city.

Four days in an unknown city and an unknown country, Remmi's enthusiasm of getting into a temporary job in a span of 96 hours created my curiosity on his lifestyle.

Remmi works for four months in his country every year, saves some portion from it for travel. He travels to meet new people in a new country that makes him a better person and offers him different experiences. And in that new country, he takes some errands and odd jobs that make his stay and food almost free and also his stay longer. What surprised me was his least materialistic need and the quest to know new people and their culture.

In those four days, he has paid ₹ 1,500 per night to a hotel for two days and in that 48 hours, he managed to convince a local family that he will offer French language coaching to their children against a barter for free accommodation for three months, a period he has the visa for to stay in this country.

On the other hand, he struck a deal to promote the heritage walk, which took care of his daily needs. But that is not all. His goal was different. He played guitar and wanted to learn the Indian music form.

In the evening, he was attending the guitar classes to add another skill for himself.

Second person: Alexendru Lambroszki from Romania came to Sangam School in Bhilwada, Rajasthan for a period of six months, through a company called Global Placement, which gives exposure to the graduate students for six months before they take up the postgraduation courses.

A management and marketing graduate, Alex was told to observe the Indian students' lifestyle for a while before he started teaching them how to manage the surroundings, environment, how to live with minimum resources, and various other life skills that can bring a change in the attitude of school children.

And in his extra time, he played football with students, teaching them team-building activities.

Alex must be around 24 years old and had been to nine countries before coming to India and worked at various designations, starting from a manual labourer in the farms to a mason on a construction site, besides at service industry like food chain and also in newspaper company among others. This varied exposure gave him a larger perspective of the global business methodologies and flip and positive side in each workplace.

Although his goal was to join the banking sector, he ensured he had enough global knowledge before he hits a permanent 9-to-5 marketing job that would shape up his entire life.

What made him stand out among the crowd was again not his fair skin but the way he has a plan for his life. He had a six-month calendar that what he will do in that school, a five-year calendar about what he wanted to achieve, an excel chart that clearly had a blueprint on which countries he wanted to visit and on which year and, finally, in which company he wanted to take up a job. And incidentally he never missed any.

Funda is that the more the exposure to several global practices, the more the mature, the young mind becomes. Allow our younger population to have 360-degree exposure in all fields to help make better choice in their life.

□

33

Start thinking positive and see how things fall in place

Eha Kern was showing a film on rain forest. Images of bright-coloured birds, wildlife, snakes and insects raised the enthusiasm in the 10-year-old's classroom. Every pair of eyes in that class was glued to the television screen. Suddenly, the documentary showed very disturbing scenes, like rain forest on fire and animals running helter-skelter. Eha then explained them how the home of hundreds of species of flora and fauna is being stripped bare by loggers to make furniture and build houses.

Smiles suddenly vanished among the children of Fagervik School in rural Sweden and they felt bad. Some faces creased into a frown. A nine-year-old boy, Roland Tiensuu, said, "Is it true that rainforests are disappearing?" and the teacher nodded in affirmative and the second question from him was, "Why can't we buy some rainforest and protect it from loggers and fires?"

The classmates laughed and said, "We have enough money to buy only candies."

Delighted that her pupils were so engaged with their project work, the next week Eha invited American tropical biologist, Sharon Kinsman to visit the school. Sharon was well known for her work in Costa Rica and the kids were overawed by the pictures she showed them on the rainforest in Monteverde, Costa Rica. She told them that more than 400 bird species live in the forest, along with a similar number of butterfly species and 500 types of trees. Monteverde (green mountain) is also the only home in the world for the golden toad, a creature that seems to glow in the dark.

Sharon then showed them the harsh reality – of loggers with chain and saws cutting down trees. She explained that some people in Monteverde were trying desperately to buy land so that more trees wouldn't be cut by loggers. It was the early 70s, and some land had already been protected, but much more funds were needed to preserve the rest. Land was cheap there, she said – only about $25 per acre.

Roland's idea now seemed possible. He and his teacher passed a hat to collect money from the gathering since the gathering had parents and guardians and they collected just $500—enough to buy 20 acres of land.

Next day, spurred on in the knowledge that they could buy a rainforest after all, the children raced into the class, full of ideas for further fund-raising activities to buy 10 hectares of rainforest. The students – around 60 of them – painted pictures, made greeting cards and held a cake sale, raising enough money to buy four hectares of the Monteverde forest.

Spurred on by their success, Eha shared the story with her colleagues. The other classes soon came up with their own ideas to raise money. With plays and pony rides, one event led to another and the word spread to other schools across Sweden.

By the mid-70s, a total of $100,000 was raised. Inspired by the students, the Swedish government gave a grant of $80,000. After a newspaper article was published about their efforts and a television report aired, children from 44 nations joined hands and raised more than

$2 million, which the Monteverde Conservation League used to buy nearly 33,000 acres of rainforest.

The funds were used to establish what is now known as the Children's Eternal Rainforest (CER), which is the home to about 5 per cent of the world's birds, 3 per cent of the world's butterflies; and 3 per cent of the world's ferns. To put size in perspective, the CER covers only 0.0048 per cent of the Earth's land surface, but it contains 5 per cent of the world's birds.

Funda is that a small positive thought in a single child today has given birth to a home for thousands of lives. Just think positive and see how everything falls into its place.

□

34

Don't allow our urban lifestyle to affect children's health

Rahul is ten years old. He gets up at around 7:00 a.m. to reach his school at 8:30 a.m. that includes 30 minutes of travel. He is the most bright student of a modern convent school. No sooner he gets up from his bed and brushes his teeth, he takes his books in his hand. In fact, the parents have to tell him to attend family get-together, ask him to come out from his room for a walk, for shopping in the mall etc., since he keeps himself busy studying as his target has been to get in the top ten slots of the school's state examinations to be held in 2017 summer (name changed on request).

Which parent will not be happy to have such children at home? He is academically brilliant, and a pride of their home, society, school and peers.

He has always been first from his first standard and has been the best class head, school's head boy, top scorer, and managed to get over dozen trophies from many competitions, including spelling bee, Bournvita quiz contest among them.

But there is a bad news. His physique that was calculated on six fitness parameters, like sprint capacity, endurance, flexibility, lower and upper body strength, abdominal strength and Body Mass Index (BMI) had been lower.

He is not the only one. Every two kids in this country out of five don't have healthy BMI, at least one in every four kids of this country does not have adequate endurance capability. One out of every four kids does not have the desired flexibility. Upper body strength of Indian kids though bit better, the lower body strength is weak, the overall strength including the abdominal strength is low when compared to international standards.

In a survey conducted for over six years by Edusports, an organisation apparently formed to create 'physically educated' children, on 1.48 lakh students aged between 7 and 17 years from 87 cities across India, has revealed some startling facts, which have made the parents sit up and take notice of their children's health report cards.

Interestingly, the survey pointed out that though the parents are completely aware of the exercises that children need to put each day, the health report card of the next generation has become the cause of concern. Other issues like unavailability of open spaces to play, too much stress on academics and badly maintained playgrounds in every city are starting to show in the kids' health report cards.

The lack of physical activities, like outdoor games and exercises, has left many urban children with lower Body Mass Index (BMI) and endurance levels. Fitness levels of these children are much lower than the standard measures. Complicating the problem is the lack of physical education classes and includes sports education in schools.

The survey indicates that since the students play fewer games that involve running, it results in poor lower body strength. Parents, particularly those who spent some time abroad where the physical fitness is taken seriously, understand this issue and are ready to spend money but look for clubs where their kids can get such facilities.

In India, in a class meant for physical activities, there are a few who are playing and the rest become audiences. The ones who are stronger generally are the lucky ones who get to play. Though we do not stop teaching an academic subject if the child is weak in it, we fail to apply the same rule when it comes to sports and the direct fallout is: poor health card.

Funda is that to create an overall – healthy next generation, schools, parents and policy-makers must ensure that the overall education system must be inclusive of physical education.

□

35

Good environment offers good results

Year: 2008. Location: A 122-year-old Government Vocational Higher Secondary School for Girls in Nadakkavu, a small town at Kozhikode in Kerala, meant for mainly fisher-folk families' children.

The dilapidated school, with broken or no furniture in classrooms, leaking classrooms, dirty washrooms will put off any student. The chipped off dirty walls, pillars holding on to the roof as if it is telling you "am tired and I want to lie down and rest", roofs with no roof tiles, leaky classrooms in rainy seasons, every inch of an open area is filled with overgrown weeds, pockmarked with rocks and shrubs, nine washrooms for over 2,000 girls, with many of them without doors or running water, the school was the best in the worst.

The demoralised teachers and staff members shudder to enter the school while the students detested going to school. Visiting this place was more of a punishment.

Parents were withdrawing their children in droves and the staff vacancies never got filled because there were less students and those left were failing in exams and getting dropped out. Probably, this picture will give you enough points to ponder why there are dropouts in the government-run schools.

Hoping to improve the conditions, a local legislator, Pradeep Kumar, opened the first chapter of change in

2008 by utilising a portion of the development funds of ₹ 10 million granted to local legislators and set about repairing the crumbling school.

His request for help to people in ISO and Infosys culminated with a telescope and some multimedia equipment but that was not enough to save the school as it needed a lot more and urgently.

Now move to UAE. The ₹ 28.8-billion turnover company, KEF Holdings is run by a businessman Faizal E. Kottikollon and his wife Shabana Faizal. The couple had established the Faizal and Shabana Foundation in 2007, keen to do something for the community, or to say pay back to the city where they come from and it was coincidently Kozhikode in India.

Now come back to Kerala. The couple didn't even think twice when they saw the school and granted ₹ 160 million for its makeover.

Old structures that could not be salvaged were knocked down and the modern ones built. The relatively better structures were spruced up. Some heritage structures were preserved and the new ones were designed in a such a way as to blend with the old. In just over a year, the school morphed into a modern institution with state-of-the-art educational facilities and play areas.

The changes are visible right from the entrance of the school. The broken gate and run-down wall have given way to a boundary wall with a large gate manned by two security personnel at all times – a rarity for the state's government schools.

The school also boasts of a 132,000-sq-ft landscaped garden, a library with around 25,000 books and an 18,110-sq-ft AstroTurf multi-purpose playing field for athletics, football and hockey. The new sports complex has a 13,000-sq-ft indoor stadium, wood-floored basketball and badminton courts, and spacious changing and locker rooms for students.

With digitally equipped classrooms, modern laboratories for physics, chemistry and botany, 92 spotless toilets, a corporate-style kitchen and dining hall that can seat about 600 at a time, the school is an example of how a couple's initiative to make a difference in the field of education can change the lives of thousands of students and their families. Today, they have 81 teachers for 2,497 students and 92 percent of the students in their final examinations this year scored A+ grade, a huge success by any standard.

Funda is that if you change the environment, the success result will jump multiple times. But you need a large heart like Faizal's to do that.

□

36

If your determination is stronger, even destiny will be ready to mend its ways

Hasmotullah Momin weaves gamchhas, which means towels in Bengali, in his hometown situated in Birbhum district, which is around 190 kms away from the capital city of Kolkata.

He would always travel on foot to the neighbouring villages to sell his weaves. A pack of four gamchhas priced ₹ 120 would fetch him a profit of ₹ 25-30 instead of the ₹ 10-15, if he supplied them to a wholesaler. If he had been an educated person, he could have easily written a full dictionary out of one word called 'struggle'. To that extent, he has experienced struggle in his life with family supporting him like a rock and he supporting them back.

Zahiruddin Momin, known as Zahir to all his friends, was never allowed to get dropped in his school. Zahir always helped his father to weave gamchhas. But his father never allowed him to take his studies lightly. The senior Momin would put extra work to ensure the junior does well in life.

All through his life, he has seen two things – on the one hand his father's hard work and, on the other, his peers suffering from one ailment or the other and continue to suffer due to the lack of a paediatric medical professional, who can treat them at low cost. But somehow setbacks are always part of the poor family. Despite Zahir passing out from school with flying colours, despite he getting prepared for the common medical entrance examination and despite a coaching class coming forward to teach him free, fate had different plans.

Two years before when he was on a bus travelling to Suri, the capital of his Birbhum district, to write the entrance examination, the bus met with an accident. The young man, who had prepared for the test injured his right elbow and was unable to write the papers as well as he had expected to. He reached the examination centre about 30 minutes late and since the elbow kept hurting as well, he performed bad.

Though he ranked poorly, his father did not deny him a second chance. When he was preparing for his second attempt, there were moments when he didn't feel like studying since poverty was striking on his face. He felt like going out, work and get some money to support his family. But he controlled it looking at the hardship his father and their family had taken to bring him up till here. That was what motivated him and made him strong to take setbacks on his stride.

Now fast forward to November 2015. Zahir is standing outside a mall in Kolkata and resisting his temptation to enter a movie hall and watch a movie of his choice. It would cost him ₹ 80. In fact, that will help him at least photocopy a book if he cannot buy it, since he has become the first-year MBBS student at the College of Medicine and Sagore Dutta Hospital in Kamarhati, around 14 km way from the mall where he is standing.

He kept requesting his seniors in college not only to lend books but also the skeleton-set needed for the first-year students. Zahir's seniors then referred him to the teachers who advised him to apply for scholarships. And few days back he climbed up the Science City stage to receive the Nirmal Chandra Kumar Memorial Scholarship for Knowledge Enhancement presented and supported by media and corporates. He is confident that in the next five years, a paediatric doctor will emerge to support the next generation's destiny as far as their health is concerned.

Funda is that if you are strong-willed, even destiny will be ready to bend a bit and pave way for the better future.

□

37

A school can promote and disseminate the right information for your product!

Recently, I had a meeting in a restaurant that was specialised in sea food, although they serve for others. Over lunch, as my meeting was on, I could see a bunch of foreigners, some of them Japanese, listening to an Indian with rapt attention. The young man lecturing about Japanese seafood delicacy called Sushi and all the listeners openly appreciated his knowledge which was apparently more than Japanese themselves.

When I approached him to enquire his ability to get so much of knowledge on sea food industry, he said he was a student of 'school of fish' from UK. "Wow I was not aware any such school," I said.

He added, even in India the first of its kind, called 'school of fish' has recently started at Kochi in Kerala and had held its first one-day workshop this month where 40-odd enthusiasts – hobby chefs, senior chefs, homemakers, and kids – came to learn the art of sushi from the experts. In fact, he was one of the participants.

For a generation that has renegotiated its tea and coffee culture and, to a great extent, the way food is consumed, Farak Javed, the young and inventive director of Abad Fisheries, a century-old seafood company, has come up with novel ways to bring seafood and fish to the fore of social imagination, much like the brew.

In August this year, Abad School of Fish began its operation with a tie-up with Billingsgate Seafood Training School of Fishmongers' Company in UK.

In 1998, Fishmongers' Company was instrumental in establishing the Billingsgate Seafood Training School (BSTS), with the assistance of the Corporation of London and the London Fish Merchants' Association.

The founding principles of the school were threefold: to demonstrate to children and young people the importance of seafood in the diet; to keep alive the fish-mongering skills now widely lost to the industry; and to promote to the public the health benefits of seafood – all of these aims are achieved daily, thanks to the busy and involved cookery courses offered by the school.

BSTS has proved a catalyst in providing the motivation for several new businesses as a result of people wishing to begin a career in the industry attending one of the industry start-up courses, such as 'Get into Fish Mongering'. The school is also a part of the National Seafood Training Academy and is, therefore, at the forefront of helping to develop the new Modules of assessment for younger population that is keen to learn about seafood.

Sensing the existing disconnect between the fish and the fork, be it in hygiene or product accountability, Faraz finds consumers lacking in awareness on the wealth of fish available. Many fish are shunned by fisherman themselves because of their strange appearance. These are apparently tasty with excellent meat. The school management believes that there is misinformation or lack of information on them, which is what the school wants to bridge.

Abad School of Fish will be operational early next year. The courses will range from short one-day workshops to more elaborate and detailed courses led by experts. Certificates will be issued. Classes will be open to all enthusiasts, be it fishermen, chefs, homemakers, children or professionals. However, a specialised workshop on fish will be held every month.

Wine-makers and liquor manufacturers already run schools for disseminating the right information about their products and this thought being applied to fish is certainly new to India, though it is present abroad.

Remember National Egg Coordination Committee promoting egg-eating; now fish-promoting school.

Funda is that starting a school for product promotion and for the right information dissemination is certainly a win-win situation for industry and the product users.

□

38

Retirement is only for job, not for life

Her parents were flower-sellers; in fact, even today they are still selling flowers and bringing home a meagre income. They did not have money to send their daughter for further education after 7th. But in 2015, their daughter, Monika Bhavshar, is studying electronics and communication branch in engineering at Ahmedabad College. She managed to get everything – from a cycle to reach school and college to laptop, besides books and a education material for her graduation purpose.

Sagar Khai is currently doing his final textile technology course in engineering but had no money to even pursue his high school some years ago. Jaydeep Patel was in H.Sc. and didn't know what subject to pursue. After a long counselling session he pursued his career in B.Sc. and wanted to become a lecturer in Mathematics. And today he is almost at half way mark to fulfil his dream.

Mittle Patel did BCA and is now supporting her family financially while just a few years ago, the family could not support her even in school education.

There are scores of others, some doing commerce graduation along with CA, some doing engineering and many doing their choice of education.

They all have one thing in common. They were either helped, coaxed, counselled, or taken care of by an organisation called "Dada Dadi ni Vidhya Parab."

Parab in Gujarati means it is a place where water is distributed free of charge to any passerby, more particularly in hot summer. It is like heaven to quench the thirst and move ahead.

In 2004, having nothing to do much after retirement, a couple thought that their knowledge learnt all over their life should not go waste. They decided to put their knowledge not with those who can afford to buy it but for those who long for good teaching but have no money to pay. The couple started a 'Parab' not for quenching thirst but for quenching the knowledge thirst of the poor children who have no place to go. And Deepak and Manjari Buch aptly named it as "Dada Dadi ni Vidhya Parab."

Started with two students, the cause went like wild fire through mouth publicity, more faster than WhatsApp of these days, and in the first year itself, the number touched nearly 100 students taking educational help with them. Currently, they have 180 needy students.

Manjari Buch takes Maths and English for primary students while Deepak Buch takes care of the seniors' requirements.

Apart from the bookish knowledge, they paid huge attention to the culture, their behaviour with family members, and their care for larger aspect of the society. Being operated from their home, the organisation selects only those children who have the drive for study but need some push to excel but the primary rule is that they need to be poor, who cannot afford any coaching.

Providing self-confidence and an all-round personality to become a good citizen is the goal of the couple, though they assist financially many children for higher studies. They seek assistance for this purpose from various quarters and most of the donations come from their extended family staying abroad and the large-hearted Gujarati community spread all over the state.

For Buch couple, the rule is very simple. They were retired by their employer. They could have led a peaceful retired life since their needs are minimal and they had substantial savings. But they decided against it and devoted their post-retirement life in uplifting the poor through education. And it is in the 11th year.

Funda is that one has to retire from employment as a matter of routine but the decision of not to retire from life is self-made.

□

39

Convert a classroom into a theatre sometimes to see a difference

This classroom was different. There were no young students. The menfolks were dressed in full trousers and shirts, while their peers in women were dressed in saris.

But, suddenly, in the middle of the class, the loud laughter makes us wonder what happened to these lots, which discipline others. In fact, the noise attracted young students of the neighbouring class to stand up and watch.

The noise is because these teachers were part of the 'Kalakala Vagupparai', which means laughter classroom in Tamil being held at Madurai in Tamil Nadu.

The teacher's teacher, N. Rajkumar asks all of them to close their eyes and listen carefully like a primary school teacher talking to the kids. Then he drops a coin and asks the participants to crawl and pick it up by guessing the direction of the coin from the sound. And, suddenly, 30 able bodies whose height is between 5 feet and 5.6 feet are seen crawling in the class in search of the coin. And the noise was due to that activity. And the children watching from a distance were smirking and clapping.

And for Rajkumar, he is breaking the ice and bringing his students out of their cocoons. Games such as these prepare people for theatre. And then he makes them sit anywhere they want, whichever wall they want to lean on, however closer they want to come to his table. And then he tells them that classrooms should not follow strict seating arrangement. "Teachers should experiment with the setup and layout of a classroom. It helps in bridging the student-teacher gap." And all teachers-turned-adult students agree in unison. Internationally acclaimed films on teaching like *'Beyond the Blackboard'* and *'School of Life'* were also screened for the teachers at the workshop.

Theatre is not just about acting on a stage. It's an inseparable part of life. On a daily basis, all of us are acting every now and then – through our expressions, voice modulations and body language. The idea of theatre is to make an individual sensitive to the surroundings and as expressive as possible. And there is nothing better than sowing the seeds of expression in young minds. Only then they will grow up to be responsible citizens, feels Rajkumar.

'Kalakala Vagupparai', a forum for school teachers, was formed by like-minded teachers to conduct innovative workshops on teaching methodologies. The idea was to bring together teachers who really want to make a difference to the education system. The new crops of young teachers who are thinking out of the box and want to encourage different experiments in the class enjoy this forum.

Eyes sparkle, hearts ignite and imaginations run free when these teachers go back to their schools and start narrating stories. Now the trained teachers do not come out with a set of ideas and rehearsed lines since it doesn't work like that with children.

They have learnt how to be one of them and see the world from children's eyes. Today the characters they speak are such that children could easily relate with their age group. And the attention span of the children had gone up. To hold the attention of little kids, most of these teachers have started two-way communication where the children knew that they will get a chance to talk.

Theatre in class paves way for the overall personality development of students and helps them hone skills. One of the teachers was confessing that she had seen introvert children becoming good orators in school assemblies after the introduction of theatre activities.

Funda is that sometimes classroom-turned-theatre does miracles in children's overall personality development.

□

40

God helps only those who help themselves

Janki Lal Khatri was born to a vegetable vendor family at Kota, Rajasthan. Khatri could do only two things at that tender age. Wash vessels in a dhaba besides becoming a dropout from school to reduce any expenses. That is what exactly he did.

The family shifted from 33 kms away from Kota to Bundi for better prospects but continued to do the same vegetable vendor business. His doubling up as porter in the Bundi bus stand did not improve the family condition much. Many nights the entire family either slept hungry or slept with the food cooked from the unsold vegetables, which was not enough to fill the young stomachs.

Slowly, Khatri's job profile improved a bit. He graduated from washing vessels and porter job to selling newspapers, besides getting back to school.

That was the time the family managed to marry off his elder sister to a tea vendor. Unhappy with the torture she received, she committed suicide later. Besides, there was no sign of improvement in the family's financial condition.

But Khatri believed that their family life would improve and kept studying well. His intuitive questions and his way of arguing in the class made the teachers wonder on Khatri's intelligence. They were always supportive when it came to paying his fees or his educational requirement.

Understanding his family's financial condition, the teachers also gave him lot of errand jobs in marriages and odd events that they were associated with. Khatri started earning a decent income besides concentrating on his education and he managed to complete school but stopped further education due to lack of funds.

His house was not more than a hut. With no water, no light and no washroom, his brother sold peanuts before his house and Khatri started working round the clock to lift the family's fiscal condition.

Meanwhile, elder brother finally got into Indian Army, though the salary was low, and Khatri also dreamt to follow his brother's footsteps.

But the news about his decision to stop education shook the school teachers who came to his house and convinced him to appear for medical entrance exam and had brought the application form along with them.

After he passed out in PMT, the teachers actually went around the town collecting charity for Khatri and sent him to Jaipur for counselling and then Udaipur for admission.

Next few years, Khatri never came back to his village. He worked as a proofreader in a newspaper all through the night to earn money. Later, he realised that composer gets more salary and learnt composing to earn that extra money, keeping the medical education intact.

Upon completing MBBS, he did private practice in a village near Bundi, where patients used to give him some grains, eggs, ghee, etc. as fee and not money.

Later, he got selected in Indian Railways as Medical Officer and joined at Chittorgarh.

Next few years, his job was to stabilise the family and get everyone in the family to settle down besides getting married to an assistant professor from Neemach in Madhya Pradesh.

In three decades of his working with railways, he moved to different stations, like Ujjain, Udaipur, and Indore among many before retiring as Additional Chief Medical Superintendent in 2012. After retirement, he is currently working as medical officer in a private company at Pithampur near Indore.

At least for 20 years in life, Khatri did not even know that he would become a doctor since his childhood was spent in hutment. But, he kept working hard on every opportunity given to him by fate.

Funda is that God helps everyone but he ensures only that person's success, who helps himself/herself.

□

41

If you want, you can still rewrite your fate

She was born on May 8. It is observed as world Thalessemia Day globally. It is a genetically inherited disease and cannot be passed on to another through any contact. Thalassemia major patients require life-long blood transfusion on a regular interval supported by costly medicines. But little did the child and her parents know that on the third month of the birth, she herself would be identified with Thalassemia major.

The subsequent treatment made this child completely weaker compared to any child of her age. Fortunately, her mother was a housewife while father worked in NTPC. Since she needed complete personal care, she was always on her mother's lap, more particularly when her mother is tutoring her elder sister thus exposed to the aroma of books, words, language and much more life-related learning.

At the age of six, this young girl got used to the smell of paper and her intense concentration on her mother's methodology of teaching to her sister that she almost knew everything in those books except that she never went to school.

Whenever she used to cry as a child, she was offered books and the child would immediately calm down, mostly with the aroma of the books that made her comfortable.

Though her parents sent her to school like any other child, her regular absenteeism forced her and her parents to stop her going to school after her 7th standard, thus shelving the dream of completing the school.

Then she finished her 10th and 12th as a private student and got admitted to Delhi University as a correspondence student. Finished her BA and then did double MA in Applied Psychology and English Literature, all because she had only one friend in her life – books.

Since she was fond of reading, her goal was also to become a writer. She always dreamt that her books must be read as she reads others' books. First she got exposed to blogs in which she wrote something about Samsung phone and instantly she was selected as top 20 tech-review professionals of the world by the company, though the procedure is discontinued now.

Then she got selected in an US recruitment firm but her parents refused her to join neither in US nor in their branch office at Bengaluru. She stay put in her hometown, Faridabad and the company permitted her to work from her home. Her home-office started at around evening hours to match US timing and she worked until wee hours to clinch "best employee of the company" award in the year 2014.

Meet Jyoti Arora who was convinced that her soul lies in writing and her first novel – dream's sake was published in the year 2011. Then she went on with her second novel – Lemon Girl – that she self-published in 2014. The first dwelled on psychological conflict on physically challenged people, the second one dealt with women's abuse and oppression. Both her novels have garnered positive reviews from readers as well as critics.

Other than this, she runs three blogs, won national level blog competitions, over five years of freelance writing experience, developing books for kids and abridging

24 famous English novels, like Jane Eyre, Adventures of Huckleberry Finn, etc.

Jyoti has dedicated her life to create awareness about the disease and speak on every platform possible how to prevent it during the pregnancy period. Today, she is a very confident person and believes in her identity as a novelist, blogger, tech expert, and a speaker.

Funda is that for believers, one comes into this world with some fate but your determination helps you correct it enroute.

□

42

360-degree outlook of life makes one as a responsible citizen

It was 1941. The 5th standard boy had no electricity in his poor home. The Second World War was on and the kerosene lamps could be burnt only from 7:00 p.m. to 9:00 p.m. Money and food were scarce across the country. The large joint family had five sons and five daughters and three of whom already had their own families. This last son and this young lad thus grew up seeing at least three cradles any time at his home. His grandmother and his mother were the drivers of this large contingent. Thus, the environment at home was alternated between happiness and sadness.

The young boy needed help for Mathematics but the family had no money to pay for tuition. The free tuition was given for just five students in a year which started at 4:15 a.m.

The reason for keeping it so early is that only serious students will come and attend the class. The most important condition for attending the class is that no student is permitted to enter the class without having a bath.

To send the child to attend the class so early, the mothers have to wake up even earlier, keep hot water for them if the climate is cold and help the child get ready and reach the class. And his mother never failed in that duty ever.

At 5:30 a.m. on his return from tuition, his father would take him to the Namaz and Quran Sharif learning in the Arabic school. After that, the boy will run to the railway station, which was three kms away, from his house and wait for the train to come.

The newspapers' bundle would be thrown at him from the Madras-Dhanushkodi Mail, which would not stop, since it was war time. The little boy used to collect the paper bundles and run around the town selling it and he would be the first one to distribute all his newspapers.

His eldest brother who got him to this business was the newspaper agent earlier before he went to Sri Lanka in search of a better livelihood. After distribution, the little boy used to come home at 8:00 a.m. By that time, his mother would have prepared the breakfast which was always simple but good. However, he always got some extra share since he was the youngest of all. Yet they worked and studied well together. After the school in the evening, again the little boy would go around the town for collecting newspaper dues from his clients.

One day, when all siblings were sitting together for a meal, this little boy kept asking for more rotis and his mother seldom said 'No'. He realised later through his brother that his mother sacrificed her food and starved for that day. When he heard that he rushed to his mother, hugged her tightly and realised the importance of compassion.

Periodically, he used to see Pakshi Lakshmana Shastrigal, Vedic scholar and head priest of the famous Rameshwaram temple, Rev. Father Bodal, who built the first church in Rameswaram Island and his father, who was an Imam in the mosque, discuss the island's problems and always find solutions to it peacefully.

His upbringing had hard work, time management, strictness, scarcity, poverty, sharing, love, compassion, tolerance to other religions and sacrifices – the best recipe that finally made a great human like the young boy here, whom we all know as Abdul Kalam, the former late President of India, whose 84th birthday became the birth anniversary for the first time today.

Funda is that to make the children better human beings, serve them with every aspect of humanity – good and bad – to give them 360-degree outlook of a life.

□

43

Bridge the digital divide and see the miracle in rural India

A 10-year-old girl sitting before the laptop with pride, her backbone erect straight, face gleaming with joy and started putting all her ten fingers to work like a seasoned laptop user and typed her name; but a bit slow; one alphabet after other; and finally it read as—Manju Kumari Gamati. No chance of a spelling mistake. Then she typed her father's name and then all 26 alphabets in English. Not a single mistake again.

Like the yesteryear Bollywood actresses immediately who transform the viewers to a dream scene, even Manju went to the dream world. Her face turned pink like a just blossomed lotus flower and it was a combination of shy, happiness and pride. But a huge sound of applause from people around her brought her back to the reality, which ended with some tears in her sparkling eyes – tears of joy. You may think what is new in typing own name and that too for a 10-year-old girl. Right?

Yes. It is surprising because she was a tribal girl, from a village and a two-year-old, half-constructed school, whose names are same – Jhonk Ka Bhilwada, situated 70 kms from Udaipur on a hillock which falls under the panchayat Gaonkhuda, block Khamnor, zilla Rajsamund in Rajasthan.

The village has 25 families with a total population of 80, which never went to school and had no school until two years before. This village which is 1.5 kms from the main road has never seen something called road. Manju's grandfather never saw electricity until he turned 70 and Manju herself sees electricity once in a week for a few hours for the last three years. It is a self-sufficient village for the local adivasi community, whose mainstay is farming with fruits like banana, goat milk and jaggery supporting their basic need.

All 36 students from this village are in that school and Manju was introduced to a product called "computer" just two hours before she started typing on Sunday by a set of young volunteers, who came from Haldi Ghati, a better-placed village, 40 kms away from the hillock, to teach them computers with their own laptops.

Manju was not the only child who got exposed to computer but all 46 students of that school, which included ten students from the neighboring hamlet called Nandu Khudi, were also for the first time in their life.

And the most appreciative part of the exercise was that they heard the volunteers teaching computers for the first 90 minutes and in the balance 90 minutes, they practised on the computer – some did some silly mistake but most without a single mistake.

The volunteers headed by our Dainik Bhaskar correspondent, Virendra Paliwal and his brother Jeetendra with two computer coaching class owners visited this place on the request of the school teacher, Ajay Ram, who also travelled 20 kms everyday to this school from his village to teach these kids. Though Ajay could get a job closer home, he knew that no teacher would teach under these extreme conditions and he decided to stay out for the sake of these first-generation school goers.

Today's children need not only basic education, but also the ability to deal with an increasingly complex and connected world. Thus, these youngsters' efforts to create inclusive educational solutions that address all sections of society and help transform them need to be appreciated.

Funda is that children from anywhere have natural curiosity and such activities will complement the framework of traditional schooling and these initiatives will explore new boundaries in these younger generations. And it is the modern-day method in joy of giving.

□

44

Effective teaching is like making TV commercials

Two years before when I was in Nasik on my holiday, one of my neighbours were expectant parents, waiting for the baby. To ensure that their baby is picture perfect, they put up pretty baby posters like any other young parents.

Mother learnt new language, both parents bid goodbye to their regular TV soaps and war pictures and watched Disney's classic, spent time in reading Hindi Sahitya and Bachchan's poetries and spent hours dreaming about their genius baby.

They believed if they spoke unadulterated language, the baby would be good at communication.

And last year I saw completely a different equation at their place, maybe the baby came with her own set of issues. The baby had issues like weaning plus upset stomach, which led to sleepless nights for all three among many other normal biological problems of growing up. That followed by teething and crying that made the parents to wonder at the maker's sagacity. In fact, the 24/7 clockwork precision coupled with home-keeping, tracking of bills and payments, anticipatory management of baby's need/s was taking a toll.

They felt like their vision was disappearing and wondering where those dreams had gone.

Months later, they came to me to understand the third person view on where they went wrong that they are feeling so hard-pressed in life.

As we were discussing, we saw their lovely daughter Akanksha running to the living room when the TV commercials began. Like all children, she was confining to commercials, since they are short, quick, completely different from each other and yet complete in their own sense.

There was an idea struck on us that anything we do with Akanksha has to be short, quick and fun. And on top of that, it has to be completely different.

So, the parents removed all books brought earlier and created their own set of books with one word on left side of the book and the picture on the right side of the book. All books had one ink colour and white page like TV screen.

They took five seconds to teach five words showing those exact pages and repeated that exercise six times a day. Exactly four days, Akanksha was able to pronounce hippopotamus, tiger, flamingo, ostrich and kangaroo. And in 12 weeks, the moment she saw the pictures and not the words, she could pronounce them and could read the word when pictures were hidden. In fact, the words went to her brain as pictures.

Then they created a set of another book with words that are associative. For example, set 1 had words like eye, hands, fingers, stomach, and legs. The set 2 had words like cars, auto-rickshaw, truck, ship and aeroplane and so on.

One can see a pattern in arranging the words. Either they are coming from top to bottom on your body or going from land, water to air.

Then they took her to third level of how to express her feelings. She was told how the dog is naughty; or how the moon is round; or how the flower is beautiful, etc.

The best part of these exercises was that each word was shown for one second and each word was shown six times a day and for four to six days continuously, till the child gets used to it.

And this year, 3-year-old Akanksha is reading books that a 2nd standard school kid reads.

Funda is that effective teaching should always be crisp, completely different and filled with fun like TV commercials. If Akanksha can learn, then even your kid can. But most important for parents is that they need to give lots of time and not money.

□

45

Now the world is buying 'guardian' services if you guarantee to 'guard' their children

Aditya wanted to take a two-year sabbatical and prepare himself for IIT entrance examination. He chose Kota in Rajasthan India's unofficial coaching capital for thousands of aspiring engineers and doctors as the destination. But the problem with the family they feel that "Aditya has already slipped out of their hand". This decision is the direct fallout of his rebellious behaviour.

The situation is not conducive at home since every conversation to reason out with Aditya is slowly becoming argumentative and the young lad of the house is in no mood to listen to the "old school of thought people" from home.

The family thinks Aditya has no clue of the real world while the young man has very poor opinion about the elders in the family as far as their intelligence is concerned.

So, when he chose Kota for his career preparation and was taking a break in the studies, the Sharma family members were running around, trying to pull the last straw and help Aditya to settle down in proper form.

"Nothing is perfect. Life is messy. Relationships are complex. People are irrational. In today's environment, it is very difficult for parents to send their children to a new place or unknown destination, be it even for education," says the website of Siliguri-based educational consultant Bright Education Services, since they know that there are many such Adityas in the country.

The Sharma family then identified Kamal Jain who runs "Local Guardian & Consultant" in Kota itself. Since the last seven years, his company has acted as a local guardian, who "guard" the interest of the parent to at least over 3,000 students.

The fully equipped service with over 22 people operating from every corner of that coaching class capital offers every help to their registered student in whatever areas. Each student is given a registration number and all he/she has to do is send a text message with a request and the job will be done.

The help coming with a price tag of ₹ 5,000 per annum does everything for the registered student – from getting sim card with local address to medical emergencies or situational emergencies, like getting caught with law-enforcing agencies for a mistake not done.

The idea is to offer students home environment, which will allow them to concentrate on their studies rather than fighting a situation to get some mundane things done for basic survival. Apart from that, they become the eye for the parents, who are sitting thousands of miles away from where the children are studying or staying.

They help the students because their parents would have done the same but when the same students either miss the class or go for a picnic without the knowledge of the teachers or guardians, then their act also gets passed on to the real parents for future actions.

Professional local guardians get request from the real parents to snoop on their kids. But some people make it a point very clear that they are there to help the children in the city and not to spy on them, while some extend snooping services for extra money.

The professional local guardians are very clear that any permission for their night-outs and social life has to come from the real parents and they will not intervene in that area.

Funda is that new demands are emerging, and there are plenty of business opportunities without any much capital investment to meet those demands. The only condition is watch the undercurrents and make the first move before others enter it.

□

46

School projects must add value and skills that make students responsible citizens

As parents, we all want our children to grow up to be responsible citizens and good people. We want them to learn to feel, think and act with respect for themselves and for other people and the environment. We want them to pursue their own well-being, while also being considerate of the needs and feelings of others. Ultimately, we want them to recognise and honour the democratic principles. We want them, in short, to develop strong character.

So, we as parents concentrate on academic achievement and professional success but fail to pay more attention on moral strength and civic virtue which is the foundation of life.

But students of New Grace English School at Meeta Nagar at Kondhwa in Pune set out a perfect example of how to make students into future responsible citizens.

On the one hand, the civic authorities were unaware of garbage piling up in the localities and, on the other, local residents were not caring about it, but the students from class VIII to X took up the cause.

Md. Muzakkir Shaikh along with his school friends took this initiative and presented the idea with a plan of action to their school teacher. Muzakkir is also an active member of Bala Jannagraha, a non-governmental organisation (NGO), where children work together for civic activities.

Appreciating Muzakkir's initiative, the teacher took up the issue with Zaki Shaikh, chairman of the school who was impressed with their plan and decided to support them. The school unanimously decided that this activity is the best way for the children to understand the concept of being a responsible citizen, instead of teaching the same in the class with the help of books.

Then a meeting was scheduled between the select students and the ward officers at the Pune Municipal Corporation (PMC), who were unaware of the garbage pile-up. The ward officer responsible for the area, Alice Pore, then instantly gave her mobile number and asked the students to contact her whenever the collection vehicle goes missing for long.

During the meeting and subsequent days of collection, the students realised that it is very important for the residents of the area to participate in the activity if they wanted a cle[illegible]nvironment, besides segregation of wet and dry gar[illegible]

Then th[illegible]ok out a rally as planned earlier to create awareness among residents of the locality about the importance of waste segregation and the significance of disposing it in a judicious way. The students went on a door-to-door campaign to educate the residents.

Repeated campaign by their students kept the civic body on toes and residents slowly started adhering to the students' requests when it came to disposal of garbage. In fact, after this initiative, some students said that cleanliness can be achieved only with citizens joining hands with civic bodies.

Today, the locality is much cleaner and gives a look of a countryside in some developed nations, while the students have taken turn to keep a watch if garbage collection vehicle is not seen on time. Kondhwa as a locality generates 27 tonnes of garbage on a daily basis. It is not possible to deploy huge manpower to segregate the garbage and the waste disposal machinery does not allow the civic body to dispose them off in the mixed form, thus leading to the garbage to overflow on the roads. But thanks to these school students, which has given a different look to the entire locality.

Funda is that, such hands-on projects help them acquire values and skills that they can rely on throughout their lives and make them responsible citizens.

□

47

If you are very good, even world's top 5% take note of you

Story 1: Bhopal-based Harsh Songra was just 11-year-old eight years before. He was diagnosed with dyspraxia. It is a form of developmental coordination disorder affecting the motor coordination in children and adults, sometimes affecting speech. This means children may find difficulties in self-care, writing, typing, or riding a bike. In adulthood, it continues in learning new skills, such as driving a car.

Although the exact cause of the disease is unknown to the medical world even now, it is believed that the messages from the brain are transmitted to the body in a disruptive manner, which affects the person's ability to perform certain movements in a coordinated way.

Although the disease is not curable, with time, the child can improve and the earlier the child is diagnosed the better and faster his/her improvement in life will be.

Harsh saw his problem not with self-pity but with determination to help parents identify the problem in their children at the earliest age possible, if it is there. He seldom wanted the younger kids to go through what he went through.

In January 2015, at the age of his 19th year, this boy from Bhopal School of Social Sciences, has developed an

Android app called "my child" which can predict if a child is likely to suffer from a development disorder in flat 45 seconds. The app's calculations are made by working with basic parameters like a child's height, weight and gender.

Songra's launch coincided with Facebook's 'FB start program', which was promoting and supporting new technology ideas from various parts of the world and Harsh's app was selected as one of them. He was called later to make his presentation at a Facebook event this year in Bengaluru, where his talk attracted the attention of none other than Facebook's Chief Operating Officer (COO), Sheryl Sandberg. She had sent him a friendship request on his Facebook account later!

And in her Facebook account, she said about him that "we are supporting developers like Harsh, who have great ideas but cannot always access the resources they need." After this Facebook request, Harsh's life has gone through a sea change and responsibility has increased manifold to create something newer for the emerging world.

Story 2: Deepak Ravindran is from a small town called Kasargod in Kerala and a college dropout. When he entered the Lal Bahadur Shastri College in his hometown, he experimented with his own startup in 2007. Fortunately, for him, his company was picked up by IIM, Ahmedabad for an Accelerator program, in which they paid him ₹ 3.5.lakh as funding with a condition that he needs to move to Gujarat.

For a whole month, the family and friends thought he got admission in IIM, Ahmedabad.

The choice was very clear – College or IIM's accelerator program. He and his three friends dropped out of college and moved base. They launched innoz, an SMS-based search engine and later they launched Data lording-over voice technology. But in 2014, Deepak combined both and launched Lookup. Lookup is a hyper-local messaging app that allows businesses to connect with their local consumers.

And, instantly, two people picked up their shares in his company – Infosys' Krish Gopalakrishnan and Twitter co-founder, Biz Stone. Krish and Biz know one thing that the technology is moving hyper-local and it is better to move faster there. And today this dropout is the largest recruiter of his college.

Funda is that if you are really good in your area of work, then the world's top five percent of people who look for new ideas, new businesses will always pick you up without any hesitation. But you need to be really good.

□

48

Technology can take a good teacher anywhere without travelling

Kalu Singh is a primary school teacher in a secondary government high school situated six kms away from his village, Gehuwara at Dungapur district in Rajasthan. The village has a little over 60 houses with 300 people living in it. But the mobile connectivity is far more than perfect: in fact, better than roads in those areas.

Kalu Singh is a happy and satisfied person with his meagre income but what was bothering since the start of this academic year is that how his son Mohit who is in 10th standard will face the board exam without any external help, since Kalu himself is not good in those subjects.

His fellow teachers cannot help his son with extra coaching since they stay in different villages. Gehuwara has no coaching class since it does not make any business sense for such small population and thus students appearing for any state or competitive examination seldom get any help.

Mohit is one of the millions of students living in rural India who are denied access to expert faculty, have very little time for self-study since travelling to school and back takes maximum of their spare time and they do not have financial muscle to shift to cities to get the best coaching for such examinations.

On the other hand, Surbhi Bhagat from Jaipur realised this disconnect well when she herself was a student of 8th standard in 1997 at Kendriya Vidyalaya. She herself spent travelling over 20 kms a day attending different tuitions and had no time for revision or self-study.

After doing her computer engineering and working with IBM as SAP consultant, she branched out to create a solution for the problem she faced in her school days. She started Bhagatsir.com, an education portal, to develop and deliver all subjects of class 6 to 12 in both Hindi and English medium.

Bhagatsir.com offers e-learning chapterwise, Question and Answerwise, with sample papers. Besides, a special service is offered to students which makes learning, retaining and recalling any information learnt through this system faster.

Kalu Singh subscribed to Bhagatsir.com and is seeing a huge change in Mohit since the last three months except that his 3G internet charges have moved up anything between ₹ 2,000 to ₹ 3,000 per month, which is pinching his pocket.

Surbhi understood that it is an irony that good teachers do not go to places, where they are most needed and bright students' education's aspirations gets killed very early without even giving them a small push.

Surbhi Bhagat's idea is well received by students at the remotest place and her company is already in coordination with Rajasthan state government in doing a pilot project involving over 200 schools, which has over 2.5 lakh students. Students from the nearest places like Dausa in Rajasthan, Government Middle School in a village like Badraan in Udaipur district to far-off places, like Ranchi in Jharkhand and the remotest place of West Bengal are part of this technology just because it teaches them in their language and as many times as they want, since they have to only connect to the net and click on their computer to get their questions answered until they are satisfied.

Bhagatsir.com has targeted schools equipped with computer and internet in the remote places of Rajasthan while talks are being held with other state governments like Haryana, Bihar, Arunachal Pradesh and Chhattisgarh.

Funda is that technology can take any good teachers to any corner of the world without moving them physically.

□

49

Try social entrepreneurship to get make your career canvas larger

Students enrolled in at least ten schools near a suburb called Mankhurd in the middle of the dream city, Mumbai are forced to wade through a 25-metre-long nullah everyday to make it to their class. The alternative, a 1.5 km detour, is out of question, which takes 45 minutes more, for the locals who prefer to brave sludge containing industrial waste, sewage and garbage, often at the risk of contracting skin infections.

Children who live in the locality have no option but to cut across the drain to reach schools and coaching centres in the entire colony that houses over 20,000 people.

Most of the families take this route at least six times a day since every facility for running a normal household is on the other side.

Many children often report skin infections which not only refuse to go away but some times their scratching skin becomes the issue of mockery in the school.

A bridge over the gutter has been the political issue in every election, maybe Assembly or civic, but authorities seldom paid attention to the basic need for years close to three decades.

Social workers in the area also claimed that crossing the nullah has become the immediate cause for high dropout rate of students below seven years of age in the locality which currently stands at 20.76 per cent.

Then came a 17-year-old messiah, a student himself, after reading the plight of his fellow students from another suburb called Thane.

The student, Eshan Balbale moved by their daily struggle got a 25-metre-long bamboo bridge built over the nullah in flat eight days.

The four-feet wide and 100-feet long overpass that got opened few days ago has signboards informing students that "not more than 50 people should cross at one time".

It is a different story that Eshan belongs to a well-to-do family, who wanted to pursue aviation as his career, yet he paid attention to the need of the weaker sections staying around him. Another surprising factor is that his father had earmarked large sum of money for the ensuing 'Dahi handi' festival to be held, which is eventually celebrated with pomp and gaiety in his suburb that has taken a political overturn over years. Contributions from rich families are considered normal.

Since Eshan had a motive to help the students and also got a blueprint ready to build a bridge by using bamboos with a definite time frame, his father was more than happy to fund the entire cost of the bridge that amounted to ₹ 2.5 lakhs. He has taken into consideration the necessity to dismantle it, if the local civic body decides to build a concrete bridge in the future, so that the resources can be dismantled and moved to another area where it is sought.

Finally, a society that was promised moon by the people in the corridors of power and could not even provide the basic transport facility, got the same by an initiative of a school boy, who had a strong will to build a bridge. The direct fallout of this is that it got built in eight days which was denied for the last 16 years.

Funda is that if you do at least one social entrepreneurship project in your early age, it will expose you to multiple facets of the society and help you understand the pulse of the surroundings which eventually opens up different avenues for your future career.

□

50

Double-up your degree with personal experience

Aakash Ranison is like any other 20-year-old student doing his graduation. That too he is doing a distance education course from University of California from Indore in Madhya Pradesh. He knew that his degree of Bachelors in Business Administration (BBA) has taught him various management jargons, like time management, risk management, people management, resources management, and sales management among many that are typical to such course.

But what was confusing to him was how to put these ornamental words into practice and not only get a job in corporate world but also quickly move in the ladder.

Aakash, as his name suggests, decided to come down on earth from heaven; remain grounded in literal sense and embark on a thrilling trip to understand limitations of the academic programme by practically implementing them in his daily working life.

He selected an offbeat way to experience these management concepts: Cycling and hitch-hiking for close to 6,000 km! Aakash did the first lap of his learning tour by cycling from Indore to Andhra Pradesh capital Hyderabad and later to Tamil Nadu capital city of Chennai and from there to Karnataka capital of Bengaluru via Ooty and Puducherry. The return trip was from Bengaluru to Indore, he did by way of hitch-hiking.

Hitch-hiking is a process where you seek small distance 'lift' from unknown people driving on the road, which can include truck or tractor drivers. Aakash walked, cycled and hitch-hiked and covered over 20 cities in various states mentioned above, including Maharashtra, Goa and Gujarat.

Aakash's hitch-hiking expedition involved hopping on to 25 trucks, 10 vans and 52 bikes and one tractor. He also walked for 50 km apart from cycling.

This made him meet very ordinary people who became his teachers of all management subjects besides teaching him the life skills.

The reason for him to choose these two modes was to get different experiences. Aakash who covered cities and villages in the same breath got an idea of pursuing his higher studies in social entrepreneurship.

Aakash started his journey on July 8 from Indore on his cycle. He would cycle from morning till visibility permitted, after which he would seek shelter either at a petrol pump or a hotel nearby.

Though it was not very tough for him to find accommodation, sometimes he slept in the middle of a jungle in Andhra as the visibility dropped to zero.

After spending that scariest night all alone in that jungle, he came over the fear factor in life and got ready to take larger risk in life management.

Since he understood the gap between city and village, he tried to promote education to people he met. He would avoid telling people what he was doing and instead spend more time finding out what these people were doing to earn a living.

Aakash typically took small lifts rather than longer ones as it gave him the opportunity to meet more people.

Hitch-hiking is risky as you have no clue with whom you are going to be with for the next few hours and teaches you risk management, This also teaches you time management as the person with whom one is going to take his own time and thus teach some solid fundamentals. Living without money or frugal living taught resource management. The trip covered all subjects practically for him.

The negotiation skills, just-in-time management which teaches only to carry essential for that particular moment were other unexpected skills he gained.

Obviously, the trip has left Aakash far more wiser than he was earlier.

Funda is that college degrees are certainly important, but they get enriched if you personally experience those teachings with new experiments.

□

51

Teaching the professionals through videos and entertainment is a new business idea

Next month, one of the companies from the large business house of this country is organising a war game for its top officials. The top officers who generally refuse to move from their ivory towers called cabins will be taken to a small island, 130 kms away from Mumbai, where the teams will be divided into two, with one protecting the island and the other invading the same.

The game will be played for over two days in which the teams can even plan for a night attack and the teams will use all real equipment except the bullets and pistols. The take-home from this game would be: 1. How the top team can prevent their business from being invaded by competitors?; 2. What likely strategies the competitors can deploy in the market to take away your existing business?; and 3. Why it is important to remain alert all 24 hours in a highly competitive market?

Training the officials who had gone to schools and colleges some three decades ago has always been challenging for the company. More and more companies are now using the entertainment route to teach and train their professionals who are decision-makers. The only handicap in this learning is that the officials need to be shifted to another base which is time-consuming.

Taking cue from this handicap, LinkStreet, a cloud-based startup company from Bengaluru has moved the serious learning into videos to make the experiences more meaningful and powerful. The company believes that the impact of video learning is powerful, and, therefore, its potential as a service presents significant opportunities.

The company believes that if learning is personalised, gamified and consumed, as entertainment, it is the best way for corporations to train their field force too.

Organisations across sectors and from around the world are leveraging the Linkstreet platform to ensure learning that the company has made it easy and effective. The company has 30 customers across US, West Asia, Singapore and India. In India, the company is a partner to IIMs and Indian School of Business, Hyderabad, Miot Hospitals, Columbia, Asia among many other medicine-related organisations.

Since India has started providing technology speed with 3G and 4G, more people are accessing videos through mobile phones and Linkstreet allows all IIM students to access the videos with a particular password for video learning, which is more interesting than theory classes. It is also allowing individuals to host online classes through its platforms, wherein the creator can store his videos on their platform and retrieve it whenever needed.

What currently differentiates LinkStreet from others is that it allows the companies to train the new employees or the old employees in new products and in education businesses, it helps IIM and ISB by becoming their technology partner and creating entire theory into videos, which helps the students understand and consume the subject faster than before. But the company is currently concentrating only in medical and education areas, leaving the other areas wide open for competitors.

Operating on the subscription model of ₹ 200 per user for a month, the company has over 10,000 users and already attracted an undisclosed amount in series A round of funding besides raising their own fund. The company now plans to double up their staff from the current 40 employees to meet their expansion plans in other areas.

Funda is that producing entertaining videos that finally teach a course is not only a new emerging business but also profitable if the number of users goes up. And this market is completely open to any IT savvy professional. And remember, Hindi language is completely untapped.

□

52

Love for success makes even big inconveniences irrelevant

His house does not have the right atmosphere for education. Something or the other is always spread out across the house. It smells odd since the house deals with agriculture-related equipment and farming animals. Despite being away from the hustle and bustle of the city vehicle noise, the environment is noisy for various reasons. At least one can conveniently say that there is a complete absence of academic environment.

There are strong reasons for that. In the first place nobody is educated. His parents never went to school. Other family members for that matter were dropped out of the school or are taken to some odd jobs to meet hunger.

Father is a farmer, hence he is always toiling around his field hard and uses the house as the storage place. His brother runs a small grocery shop. So he also dumps his wholesale purchases in the same place. His elder brother who works as a driver behaves like any other driver due to his occupational necessity.

People and farming animal moves around the house, yelling at each other not with irritation but with instruction to get something or the other for the field work, thus leaving the place not so conducive for the now 21-year-old Narendra Laknotra.

In fact, last month's flood washed away his father's three-acre cotton crop in Rajula near Varodara and forced the family to face a huge financial loss. And the agricultural loss is something the family faces every alternate year due to some new developments.

But all these things never deterred Narendra to take to books. He scored not very impressive marks but respectable marks of 76 percent in his 12th standard. He kept improving his studies, finished graduation and entered Master degree in commerce.

But during his graduation, he did one surprising thing. He prepared himself for a Chartered Accountancy course, a course which is generally ccnsidered tough and needs lot of coaching. But Narendra studied for almost 15 hours over six months with a determination that he would change the environment of his house.

And one of the weekend this year, when the Institute of Chartered Accountants of India declared the results of CA final exams and Common Proficiency Test (CPT). Narendra cleared not only both first and second groups in the first attempt itself but stood tenth in the city of Varodara and became a Chartered Accountant.

His success is no less than the success of Rahul Agarwal (22) of Secunderabad, and Shailee Chaudhary (25) of New Delhi, who stood first or Anusha Chitturi (21) from Machillipatnam, who stood second or Deval Modi (22) from Mumbai, who stood fourth in All India Rank.

Like any other students even Narendra complained first about the lack of academic circumstances at home. But after 12th, his love for success and his hunger for becoming somebody in that uneducated family overtook everything else, thus making those small discomforts irrelevant.

Experts say that if somebody loves sleeping and sleeps for more number of hours than others, then the only way to reduce those hours is by making him or her fall in love with a new thing in life. That will automatically reduce the number of sleeping hours. And for Narendra, the hunger for academic success overtook the lack of academic circumstances and made him study 15 hours a day for six months.

Funda is that never ask children to drop a habit that you consider 'bad'. Just help them to love or like a new thing in life that you consider "good habits" and see how the old so-called 'bad' habits get automatically dropped. □

53

Environment makes your character

Story 1: The 16-year-old Aparajita Padmapani Acharya has never seen her dad, but heard about him a lot, little from her mother but more from her grandfather. He died when she was still in her mother's womb. Her family hails from Cuttack but is presently settled in Hyderabad. She is currently pursuing law. But her ultimate aim is to join armed forces.

Even her father, Padmapani Jagannath Acharya was a student of hotel management from an institute at Bhubaneswar. He was a very religious person, always carrying a pocket size book of Gita and reading it every morning and evening. Aparajita had heard several stories about her brave father from her grandfather Jagannath Acharya, who was not only a Wing Commander and was directly involved in action in the 1965 and 1971 wars, but also a great story-teller.

He has told her several stories about her religions but about his brevity, wherein her father once saved an injured Himalayan bear cub and took care of it until it got cured and then released it into the wild. She also learnt that how he was popular in all parties and social gatherings and used to attract host and guests with his ability to orate and make the evenings lighter. But what made her choose her career in army was the way he fought his last battle during the 60-day Kargil war, when he was with the 2 Rajputana Rifles while trying to capture the peaks of Tololing, a formidable task given to them to capture, which was occupied by Pakistan then. He laid down his life on June 28, 1999 while accomplishing that responsibility.

Yes she can hear that story from her grandfather any number of times. Because that story about her father, Late Major Padmapani Acharya, laying his life while guarding the nation and who was awarded the Maha Vir Chakra posthumously pushes her blood to that bravery and makes her think always to serve the nation. And that what makes her choose army as her career.

There are more to this bravery story in their family. Her grandfather's elder brother, Lt. Colonel K.M. Acharya was the first in the family to join armed forces while her father's younger brother still serves the nation.

Story 2: On Monday when Aparajita was preparing to observe Kargil diwas, students of government upper middle school in Hasiyawas village in Rajasthan staged protest against the education department shouting slogans like "Give TC (transfer certificate) if no education."

The school has 200 students and only two teachers. Hasiyawas is a remote village in Shrinagar block of Ajmer district. Despite all efforts by the state government, no teacher wants to work in such a village. The protesting students also gave a memorandum to district collector. They wanted that the school should be shut down as there is no use of running it without teachers. Most of the protesting students were girls and the land on which the school is being run is donated by the villagers voluntarily. These kind of protests are not new to Rajasthan since every year such repeated act of the students has fallen into deaf ears. The authorities are reported to be doing a 'jugad' by shifting some teachers from the nearby school, giving 'victory-relief' to the protesters.

Since the story is the same across many hamlets of this country, we produce children who see protest is the only way to draw attention and succeed.

Funda is that it is the environment that we provide that decides the character of the generation next. If you want them to be responsible, then first you try to be responsible.

□

54

GenNext way of looking at life is different from us

Story 1: She is 16, not a bright student but not dull too. All through the school, she never failed but did not score marks that took her picture to newspaper pages. But when she came to tenth standard, people around her kept drilling her that "scoring a very-high percentage is mandatory for her future career plans"; hence, she worked pretty hard and could manage to pull the marks to 78 percent in 2014-15 academic year.

The percentage was not the issue, but she was unprepared and was not aware what to do next. That led her parents to think of a new strategy as far as her career was concerned. So, S. Shivkumar and his wife Savitri, parents of Sagarikka, decided to give a break for a year from her regular school schedule and allow their child to take over the control of her own life and decide what she wanted to do further in her career. Abroad this term is called 'stepping out for a year'. Don't be surprised to get the same answer from parents of developed nations "what your son/daughter is doing this year?'

It is very easy to slide into laziness when you take a break from studies. That is why, Shivkumar and Savitri gave Sagarikka a timetable for Monday to Friday, and a separate one for the weekends. The timetable included several things including regular gymnasium, daily newspaper reading time, computer classes, several short internships in various companies, door-to-door selling of some regular products, a power-nap in the noon for 20 minutes, and finally discussing a subject with one of the parents in depth for four hours in the evening. The discussion will encompass the subject from basics to the level it is likely to reach in the coming decades.

While her school-going contemporaries were writing exams based on text-book knowledge, she was spending time visiting science fairs, and filming documentaries and by the end of nine months, she realised that she had more practical exposure. She is helping her parents to develop a mobile application called 'Pictalktionary', a visual vocabulary tool for those attempting competitive exams. Compiling her blog posts on her 'unschooled year' into a book form is the next item on her checklist. This year she has rejoined a mainstream school in Class 11.

Story 2: With an interest in biking since childhood, S. Bharath from Bengaluru quit his business after five years in the hope of a life of adventure after he realised that business was not his true calling. He basically wanted to travel the country on his bike and later start an organisation to provide consultancy services for biking expeditions. But he connected that passion with a mission.

He undertook a 20,000-km journey across three countries – India, Bhutan and Nepal – to promote literacy. Started his journey from Bengaluru on July 17 this year and supported by Rotary International during the course of his journey, he is visiting various government schools and conducting a survey on the availability of basic facilities and infrastructure. At the end of the journey, he will chalk out a plan to solve the problems at each school visited by involving Rotaract club volunteers and other civic organisations.

At the end of the week, he had completed visiting 50 government-run schools on their condition and areas of improvement. Rotary International will submit the results of this survey to relevant government organisations for action later.

Funda is that today's generation is looking at their life differently and it is our job to felicitate that new look. This does not mean they are not serious about their life.

□

55

Appreciate the 'Chhotus' who play the real life role of 'Badon Ka'

Muthu was putting his broom carefully in the less lit area of that gutter, clearing the thick, oily, grey-black sludge. His eyes were hopeful. Every few seconds he looked up for instruction. The instructor addressed him 'Thambi', which means younger brother in Tamil but real meaning of that tone is equivalent to 'chhotu' in Hindi.

Muthu is actually an underground scavenger with a difference. One could see many Muthus in the adjoining lanes of goldsmiths and jewellers' hub in every city. The gold dust from these workshop units lands up in the drains, which people like Muthu hunt out. It is then sold to dealers in the same area and in terms of yield, the returns hardly seem proportionate to the human degradation it involves.

I spotted Muthu on my visit to Marina beach at Chennai, where he was cleaning all wooden benches of the makeshift hotel until wee hours. When I asked him how his 24 hours are spent, he invited me to witness his second job.

On that night at beach, I saw a couple calling him "ye Thambi come here", pointing to an unclean table. Thambi ran on that sand with his bare tiny foot leaving the work in hand halfway, which angered another client. Thambi's carelessness earned him a hard whacking on his head from the waiter and Thambi ran back again to clean the half-cleaned table.

I could see tears on that young Thambi's eyes since he was finding it difficult to meet the peak-hour customers' demand. But the waiter spotted those tears. Waiter held Thambi's shoulder and got him closer to my table and asked "Did I hurt you?" Thambi said 'no' and instantly smiled at him. Waiter stroked his head and both got back to their respective jobs.

When I sought reason for the waiter's contradictory behavior with Thambi, he said, "Sir, poor fellow is the only earning member of the house after his father's death. His mother is unwell and looks after home while his sister is too young to even to go school."

The waiter started giving a character certificate for Thambi. He said that he is the 'anna' of the house, which means 'big brother' in Tamil, who has to ensure two square meals all 365 days for three lives. Apparently, he works in different shifts and does errand jobs to meet the need.

"If we don't massage the ego of some beach visitors, then they go and complain to tourism police about child labour and Muthu will lose his job. And that will push him and his family into worst situations" and that is the reason we behave as if we never like these young boys in our restaurants, while support them internally.

I got very emotional when he said, "Muthu gets 25 percent of all tips we two waiters collect in this restaurant, besides the salary." I went close to Muthu, patted on his back and tipped him directly ₹ 200. When I asked him what he will do with that money, in a split of seconds he replied, "I will buy slippers to my little sister since she never had one since her birth."

I instantly turned to the beach side to hide my tears because I saw an 'anna' (a big brother) in that small brother called 'thambi'. When I asked him why he is not going to school, he said, "Who will send my sister to school then?"

Funda is that there are many 'thambis' who are playing the role of 'anna' in their age of education. You can never win an argument with them.

□

56

Career is bigger than cash

Amit Parashar, a 16-year-old young boy, was my guide in Pushkar Brahma temple, where one of the morning I visited the temple. Amit was not only a smart-looking person but also a real street smart, was wearing a Levis 501 shirt, obviously a duplicate one since Levis 501 has never produced a shirt other than jeans. He presented himself very well before me as an aspiring student and has been doing the part-time job of a guide to meet his, not very many, personal expenses.

He never asked me money; kept saying whatever I can afford he is ready to accept it; he even said he will do it as a 'seva' even if I don't pay him; he was smartly positioning himself as a devoted guide to the poor pilgrims and in the process, he was slowly trapping me in his sales talk and I was willingly falling into it, since I was confident that I have nothing to lose other few currency notes, which would have made huge difference to that young boy.

He was not in a hurry. He took me around the whole temple premises and gave me a detailed historical importance of the temple.

The way he gave those unknown details on our mythological beliefs, it was certain that he has been in the business of guide for some years and not last 15 days as he claimed to me.

He took me to a shop at the entrance of the Brahma temple, the only temple of its kind for Lord Brahma in the world, where a 9th standard school boy was selling 'Prasad' material.

He was an authority in the 'Vedic' procedure on the religious practices of that temple. Both had the smartness in their face and action which was beyond their age. But both of them were completely speechless when I asked them why they are skipping their respective schools for making small change as a guide or selling 'Prasad' items for the pilgrims. What surprised me was that though the question was asked separately to them, the answer of these two young people was exactly the same; not a word of difference and it was: until yesterday I was in the school and since it is a holiday today and they are cleaning the school, we are just helping our family. A regular passerby, who overheard this conversation, said after we moved ahead a bit, "These young boys are regular to this profession and irregular to their respective schools." And incidentally both of them wanted to become a teacher in the government school at Pushkar itself. After talking to them. I knew these are completely tutored answers only for the ears of the visiting pilgrims, who sometimes pay more money out of sympathy to these self-educating youngsters. I also knew that just because they are able to narrate several mythological stories with ease to visitors, they think that they can become teachers since they believe to become a teacher, one needs good communication skills. I have no clue what economic compulsions their family have that they need to support the family financially at the cost of their career.

But it is a universal fact that when cash is chosen against career, then that horse, I mean that person, does no find himself fit enough to run a long race and grow well in career. I wish these two change that perception.

Funda is that zindagi me lambi race ka ghoda banna hai toh career pehle banaiye; paisa apne aap aayega.

□

57

Life certainly changes for good if you take the most difficult first step

First story: Shirad Shahapur is a small village located in Aundha Taluka of Hingoli district in Maharashtra which consists of 1,436 families with a population of 7,386 people. The village has lower literacy rate.

Of the 2,786 bread winners in this village, most of them being agricultural labourers, at least 95.48% of workers do not get employment for more than six months. This compels other members of the family to financially contribute.

The 16-year-old Durga Nevhal, one such extra hand in the family that used to bring ₹ 100 per day by working in somebody's field.

Durga, a student of a Zilla Parishad school, lives with her parents and her father has stopped working due to ill health and thus Durga doubles up as a worker in the farm field as well as a student in the school.

She has seen the ills of being uneducated from her two sisters, Anita and Sunita, who are now married. That is the one reason she has tailormade her study time after the school and farm work so that she does not miss any. In order to reduce this study time, she gives 100 percent attention in the school and seldom speaks to fellow students, which make it very easy for her to revise her studies in those spare times, which is too small in her packed 24 hour time schedule.

The only good thing in her family that has happened in all these years is that their 10-feet × 10-feet house has grown bigger to 20-feet × 20-feet under a government scheme. Otherwise the house is devoid of power and water connection.

Since she realised that she gets energy to study after a quick nap during wee hours, she has taken a power connection from a neighbour to whom she pays her one day salary per month – ₹ 100. And fortunately for her, the power doesn't go off when she gets the feeling to study, a rare feat in that power-starved village during the period when she appeared for her S.Sc. examination in March 2015.

And the direct fallout of that seamless hard work has finally paid off with Durga scoring 91.2 percent and in Mathematics, she scored a perfect 100, who is aspiring to become to attempt IAS exam.

Second story: Thank god the final examination in education system is always held in summer and not in winter. Otherwise Indra Lohar would have never passed her XII examination since her family has woolens to cover only three members of the seven-member family.

Living on Rajasthan's Alwar's roadside shanty and studying under the street light, eldest of five children, Indra not only scored 83.22% but she will be the first and only one to go to college from her community so far.

The 18-year-old belongs to the nomadic tribe Garia Lohar (blacksmiths) and her father gets only ₹ 100 per day, her only support being her second-hand books, limited note-books, one ball-pen and the nearby street light.

During the day, it is hard to concentrate because of the traffic and her father's noisy work. So she preferred to study tough chapters under the street light from 11:00 p.m. to 5:00 a.m. and while doing so, one of her parents would sit by her side while she solved the science equations.

After their success, both of them have received recognition from all over. In fact, both have blurred the cast divide and the thick line between rich and poor.

Funda is that if you want to be successful in life, it is you who need to take the first step.

□

58

Exams are not just test of brains but of character

At 11:00 p.m. in that lowly lit shanty, they call it is their house, at Rajajinagar in Bengaluru two people have already gone to bed – the father and son. The father had fallen from a high-rise building 12 years ago and taken to bed since then. The son has been identified with blood cancer two years before and also bedridden. And that is the reason both are asleep under medication.

At that hour, when frogs are croaking outside, the daughter is still studying while the mother comes and sits next to her. The two pairs of eyes see each other and exchange many stories. There is a loud conversation in that silence. The mother's eyes questioned her daughter, "How was your day?" and the daughter's head nodded in affection, "Good" while the left hand calls her to make her sit closer to her even when the right hand is turning the pages of Common Entrance examination books.

Mother takes her pallu and wipes her moist eyes, trying to escape her daughter's attention but the daughter has already seen it. She holds her left shoulder and kisses her cheek. For 30 seconds, both of them hug each other, even as some drops of tears from mother's eyes travel from one eye to another and make daughter's right shoulder wet.

The daughter quickly takes the glass of water her mother got for her and makes her sip.

After a loud gulp, because the tears blocked her throat, the mother removes her lip, takes the same glass and feeds her daughter. While the daughter is still studying, the mother takes her daughter's hand and keeps pressing the palm and upper arm. The young girl's eyes turn to her mother's side, wink several times, as if thanking her for relieving her pain. Then the mother shifts to the next hand and in flat seven minutes, daughter's eyes start closing down. The mother continues for a while until she is confident that her daughter's pain might have gone.

Both go to bed with their hands on each other, telling each other, "Don't worry, am there."

Meet Shalini A, the daughter. Next day morning Shalini gets up exactly at 4:30 a.m. In 20 minutes, she finishes the basic chores and rushes to five houses closeby where her job is to sprinkle water and draw Rangoli.

She is done by 6:00 a.m., after which she rushes to an office where she mops the floors and cleans the bathrooms until 7:30 a.m. and heads straight to another house to wash clothes and vessels.

Back home at 9:00 a.m. she studies until 12:30 noon for the CET exam. After some errands and quick meal, she gets into two full-time maid jobs that keep her busy until 4:30 p.m.

Then until 6:00 p.m., she is in study mode. Then she takes two more jobs upto 8:00 p.m. The load is higher for her since her mother has been assigned for her brother's and father's care, while Shalini has taken over her mother's work on herself. And Shalini's mother had taken the housemaid job since her husband became bedridden. And from 8:00 p.m. until 11.00 p.m., Shalini is back to her studies, until her body pleads for some rest.

And on this Monday, this sole bread-winner of the family of four scored 84.8 percent in the 12th science stream. She may not be the topper but different because she cleans bathrooms, scrubs utensils, cooks food and nurses ailing people while juggling studies and that too with a smile on her face, which her employer loves.

Funda is that every examination is more than a percentage score; more than a test of brains and it is actually a test of character. India has more such Shalinis who pass out with flying colours year after year. Hail them.

□

59

Managing time is the basic step to success

Time management is key for new generation's success. The 21-year-old Jitesh Sharma, a third-year chemical engineering student of IIT, Mumbai was found dead in one of the campus terraces on a Saturday evening. The suicide note, according to the police, stated that he was apprehensive about not getting good marks and thus good placement. This is despite the fact that he was the associate coordinator for IIT, Mumbai placement cell from September 2014 till date and has been exposed to various top companies and their need.

It is not that Jitesh comes from any unknown school background. He is the student of Shribaba Mastnath Public School at Rohtak in Haryana, an institution which is known for encouraging all-round development, and then later shifted to another premier institution – Delhi Public School. Jitesh was a bright and hard-working student throughout. Although various theories are going around for his extreme step, it is too early to pinpoint a reason for it, unless the investigating agencies come to a conclusion.

In September 2014, Aniket Ambhore, a fourth-year student committed suicide by jumping from sixth-floor balcony of a hostel in the campus. And

swiping all such unnatural death under the carpet is certainly under the word "rarity" which is not good for the young generation. A visible problem I can spot in the current generation is time management.

Since I stay stone-throw away distance from this institute, I see one common problem in the campus buildings as well as in the towering buildings on the other side of the Powai lake – lights are on until wee hours and shadows are seen glued to the chair with or without books or with computer/TV screen lights reflecting on window panes.

For a newcomer, this may give an impression of a city that is working hard and all through 24/7. But if you meet the same people next day morning, you will get an idea how sleep-deprived they are. Most of us are sleep-deprived and this is a proven fact today.

Work is always pressing. There is always something to finish until we sleep. Finishing studies before going to bed was a good habit then, particularly in those days when television and social media were not part of our life. But it is no more a good habit since social media has become timeless and prime time TV is now stretched until midnight. Students take more time to complete the same work we did 20 years before.

One of the surveys recently revealed that an active mobile user spends an average of two hours everyday on social media mostly checking his/her updates are getting enough likes or not.

Time has remained constant. Older generations had more time because they had fewer activities to pack in those hours, while the younger generation has too many distractions to be packed in the same hours.

The human body doesn't understand any of these. It needs sufficient rest to recover and function optimally, i.e. without stress, aches, pains and diseases. This is a fact, and irrespective of how much science and technology evolve, this will be true. A cursory look at many students across colleges shows they are hard-working, which they are. But if your eyes are trained to look a bit deeper, then you can spot the tiredness in them since their time is divided in too many issues.

Funda is that time management is the key to make the life of the younger generation easy. If TV and social media are consuming your evening hours, then shift your study time to early morning hours, since these two evils are less present at that time.

□

60

If your basics are strong, nobody can stop you becoming 'Ranchhodas'!

Remember the Ranchhodas in the Bollywood movie – *Three Idiots*? Even before he enters the hostel room, he gives an electrical shock to his seniors who ragged him by urinating on his room door. That is because his basics were clear. He knew what works and what doesn't.

Despite that clarity, the protagonist of the movie, actor Aamir Khan, is branded an 'idiot' by his engineering college professors for his practical approach towards learning without sticking to theories recorded in books. In real life, M. Abdul Razak, O. Jayapandian and V. Nagasundaram of Madurai have the same bent of mind as that of the reel life character.

Forty-five-year-old Abdul Razak dropped out of school at 7th due to acute poverty. His father, a cook, did not earn enough to educate him and five of his siblings.

He had no books to read or teachers to train, yet he has obtained recognition as an innovator solely due to practical experience gained as an electrician, which he joined after school and gradually picked up the skills of repairing electrical gadgets. Later, he progressed by learning to wind coil and started fabricating household items.

He is the recipient of a national award from the

former President of India, Pratibha Patil. He always contemplates tweaking and customising electrical, electronic and kitchen products for optimum use. He has more than 35 innovations to his credit and also holds one patent with 15 more products pending for patent approval.

Two weeks before his friend, an ironwala on the street corner approached him and was lamenting about the frequent power failure and power cost increase. He also found it difficult to get charcoal and feared about the impending damage to the customer's cloth due to the burning charcoal.

Razak learns his lessons through trial and error. His latest invention that took him over three weeks is iron box that works on LPG. He designed special nozzles to blow the fire down to heat the bottom portion of the iron box. And his friend has started using that with a 1 kg LPG cylinder.

No different is the story of Mr. Jayapandian, father of three. This 48-year-old orphaned at a young age has slogged in an iron industry and drove rickshaw in the night to eke out a living. Yet his passion for science made him to keep conducting experiments.

He has 128 innovations to his credit. They include a device that would mute the volume of television sets whenever someone rings the calling bell, an equipment to switch off the street lights when exposed to sunlight and a gadget to warn pedestrians and motorists at unmanned railway line crossings.

Nagasundaram is a 46-year-old physically challenged innovator and school dropped was one among the 10 children of a mason who grew up the hard way working in mechanic shops. Once a rat gnawed at his ration card and his family could not buy the essential commodities for three long months. This prompted him to create an electric rat trap machine.

His efforts to develop a prototype of the machine have been appreciated by the Lemelson Recognition and Mentoring Program, a joint initiative of the Indian Institute of Technology, Madras and Rural Innovations Network, Chennai. It entered into an MoU with him and granted a personal development fund.

An air lock releasing funnel designed by him was included in the National Register of Grassroots Technological Innovations maintained by the National Innovation Foundation at Ahmedabad.

Funda is that anyone can be an innovator if there is clarity in basics and foundations are stronger. Then degrees become just ornamental.

□

61

Generation Y is kind hearted; use them for a better cause

Incident 1: During my early school days, I was part of the *sarvajanik* tuition. Tuition in those days was taken as a social cause where the teacher and student were serious, resulting in 100 percent attendance from both sides though the teacher got just ₹ 1 per child per month.

And my father used to pay ₹ 2 which I used to hand over to the teacher with a pride thinking that I am paying more than other kids. The teacher on his part used to thank me while other students just got a smile in return.

Two years later, I came to know that the extra money my father paid was actually for Nagesh, my tuition partner, whose father runs a small tea stall near Nagpur Railway Station, which my father used to occasionally visit. Since Nagesh's father could not even afford '*sarvajanik* tuition', he was sponsored. It took me years to understand that a "thanks" was actually for my father and not for me. Nagesh today runs a successful eatery.

Incident 2: In 2014 summer, while having a quick lunch in one of the highway *dhabas* along the Bhubaneswar-Puri road, Suryanarayanan Balasubramanian, a student from National Institute of Science Education and Research (NISER), spotted Tehasin Khan mopping the tables and getting them ready to serve other guests while helping the servers at the *dhaba*.

After an initial introduction, Tehasin was found to be a dropout by choice, and all he dreamt was earning a few more bucks. Education never figured in his list. In 2015, brilliant Tehasin was studying in Class II at a municipal school in Bhubaneswar and was being promoted to Class IV directly.

Success with Tehasin inspired the NISER students to take up the issue of educating those from the underprivileged sections of society more seriously. With the help of Institute of Physics and IIT, Bhubaneswar they reached out to at least 50 children in a city slum. Thus Zaria, NISER's social outreach club, was formed. During the past two months, the 41 volunteers who spend three hours a week have been successful in getting 24 dropouts back to school.

Incident 3: Early this week, in one of the weddings in Wasseypur at Dhanbad near Jamshedpur, a bunch of 30 youngsters, including two engineers, a dozen teachers and other professionals were doing exactly what Tehasin Khan was doing last year – mopping the tables, cleaning the leftovers and getting the makeshift dinner table ready for the next bunch of wedding invitees. And all of them felt proud with their menial job.

These educated professionals slogged for 5 hours, attended 500 guests and got ₹ 2,000. They will spend this on books, stationery items, like copies, pencils, erasers and pens for the poor children from Katras, Dhansar and Jharia, a place where the ground spews fire, the air is thick with fly ash and life runs on rehabilitation packages.

They are members of Samadhaan – a society working for promoting education and an outfit that organises tuition classes on rooftops and open parks for children from socio-economically backward communities across the Coal Belt region and this is not the first wedding where they worked as waiters. Volunteers not only provide the tuitions, they train fresh graduates aspiring for government jobs.

Funda is that kindness has grown significantly in Generation Y and it is up to us how we spot that quality and take advantage of it to make this world even more pleasant.

□

62

Social sector is the best route for any business or career

First example: At 24, many like to go for a movie, date or to a club. But she manages executives twice her age and handles financial matters. Her days are always packed because she felt that she will never grow faster not only in wealth but also in maturity unless she does something with social impact. Her days are always packed and movie is a rarity in that young age for her.

The foundation of this thought process was laid in her mind when she was in college and helped her uncle to set up his own tea business. That is how she understood how difficult to get a skilled labourer for his business and found out that there was a huge gap between what an employer wanted and what an employee is able to give. She realised that by and large, the employer loses three months of wages to get that labour understand the basics of his/her business.

She graduated and got a job in a beverage company, where she worked for a while to understand the labour related issues in an organised sector and waved a goodbye before she decided to co-find 'Ace Development Skills' with her parents in 2012.

Meet Shruti Vinod and at 24 reaching out to people at the bottom of the economic pyramid is her mission statement. Her company uses skill development to help rural and urban youth to find employment. First, they started training them in farm related work and then slowly moved into hospitality, beauty culture and even mobile repair.

Second example: Tanushree Goel is a student. When she was at 12th standard, she did a community project for villagers just on the outskirts of Jaipur city in Rajasthan. She formed a cooperative to sell their vegetables and also had set up online facilities for a minimum purchase of ₹ 250. Gradually, she helped the farmers build their capacity, understand the need of the consumers and ways to meet them. In fact, three years down the line, they are on their own. She was not paid for that hard work then, because it was a project.

Now, fast forward to year 2015. She has been offered $3,00,000 (₹ 1.81 crore) scholarship by Columbia University, where she will study International Relations and Political Science. Her scholarship amount covers tuition fees, food and lodging, books, personal expenses, health and other insurances and annual return air ticket. Thanks to the project that gave her the edge in the global competition, wherein thousands of students competed with each other for scholarships.

Apart from her, other Jaipur residents like Aman Kapoor, Devansh Sand and Saksham Bhandari also got 100% scholarships to pursue their four-year graduation course at premier universities in the US. They were rewarded for their leadership skills while handling projects in the social sector besides consistent performance in academics.

Third Example: In his college, he is always teased as 'guru' because he kept advising people how to 'live'. But at 21, he had the option to go abroad for graduate school or work for my family's business. Like any other collegian, he also played cricket but could have taken it professionally but he always wanted to start something that would help change people's lives.

At 23, Sarvesh Shashi's studio was named 'Zorba' at Chennai, which offers 14 different kinds of yoga and believes in "guiding people to live, and not just to exist".

Funda is that people take them seriously when they find young people operating in social sector that paves way for a great business and career.

□□□